EAT...THINK...HEAL

One Family's Story of Discovering
the Healing Powers of Food and Thought

MARGARET BRIDGEFORD

BALBOA.
PRESS

A DIVISION OF HAY HOUSE

Balboa Press books may be ordered through booksellers or by contacting:

Balboa Press
A Division of Hay House
1663 Liberty Drive
Bloomington, IN 47403
www.balboapress.com.au
1 (877) 407-4847

Because of the dynamic nature of the Internet, any web addresses or links contained in this book may have changed since publication and may no longer be valid. The views expressed in this work are solely those of the author and do not necessarily reflect the views of the publisher, and the publisher hereby disclaims any responsibility for them.

The author of this book does not dispense medical advice or prescribe the use of any technique as a form of treatment for physical, emotional, or medical problems without the advice of a physician, either directly or indirectly. The intent of the author is only to offer information of a general nature to help you in your quest for emotional and spiritual well-being. In the event you use any of the information in this book for yourself, which is your constitutional right, the author and the publisher assume no responsibility for your actions.

Any people depicted in stock imagery provided by Thinkstock are models, and such images are being used for illustrative purposes only. Certain stock imagery © Thinkstock.

Print information available on the last page.

ISBN: 978-1-4525-2878-6 (sc)
ISBN: 978-1-4525-2879-3 (e)

Balboa Press rev. date: 05/18/2015

We write about that which we wish to learn.
I thank my family for the opportunity to learn.

Dominating nature is an obsession for humans.

We are paying the price.

Come with me as I tell you my story—our family's story—of food and farming, of health and ill health, and of understanding the healing powers of the universe and the choices we really can make.

Contents

Part One

The threads of our story began more than a decade before I was born—when man was putting his stamp on the earth in a more cumbersome way than ever before. It permanently changed our intricate relationship with our planet. The year was 1947. It was a seemingly innocuous decision that altered man's place on earth.

That date heralded the decision to convert a wartime weapons factory in Alabama, USA, into a fertiliser factory. There was a long history of development leading up to that decision and a string of consequences that have occurred as the result of it.

This story is a journal, from a twenty-first-century perspective, of man's relationship with himself and with planet Earth. The journal is through my eyes—a modern, educated woman from a western society, whose existence is woven intricately into the web of modern life.

Chapter 1

Our Farm, Our Family, and the Food We Grow

Fast forward fifty years after that 1947 decision, to 1997 and to the other side of the world, Down Under on the Darling Downs in Queensland, Australia, home to some of the world's most fertile farm land. It was also home to our farm and our family. Here you can witness modern agriculture at its supreme best. Vast tracts of land proudly show off their immaculate rows of grain crops. They are all planted using large, powerful tractors pulling precision machinery more than ten metres wide, together worth hundreds of thousands of dollars. The planting technique is state of the art. It allows the seed to be drilled straight into the ground through last season's leftover crop stalks without disturbing the topsoil, to avoid the loss of precious moisture. The seeds are coated with an insecticide to stop ants from eating them, and fertiliser is applied either in granular form or as a gas drilled into the soil. The plants are carefully monitored for unwanted weeds or insects during their five to six months of growth. These pests are then controlled with the required chemical at the appropriate time to give the plant its best possible growing conditions.

Tracing the boundary of this immaculate, industrialised grain farm is a concession to Mother Nature. Land that could otherwise be planted to crops has been handed over to plant a greenbelt of trees, designed specifically to link with the trees beside the creeks, thus providing a nature path for local wildlife from one watercourse to the next.

Located on the same farm is a cattle feedlot, where the cattle are fed a carefully designed ration of grain and roughage, combined with the appropriate medication, to avoid bloating or sickness and to maximize weight gain. These cattle are fed twice a day for between three and six months before being sold to Australian customers or exported to Japan.

Both aspects of this business, the crops and the feedlot, work together to buffer the variable income so familiar to those who rely on farming as their livelihood. When grain prices are high, the profit is made from the farm. At these times, the feedlot carries fewer cattle because it is too expensive to feed them. When grain prices are low, the profit is made by fattening the cattle and selling them for a higher price margin per kilogram of body weight. There is no guarantee that the cattle market will be buoyant just because grain prices are low, but cheaper grain means one less variable to have to worry about in this highly intensive, integrated farming operation.

Ours was a successful business by any economic standards. It was highly valued farming land, servicing a debt of 25 per cent of the asset base and vertically integrating its operation. It supported three generations—grandparents, parents, and grandchildren. We also employed four other families on a permanent basis, plus other local people and farming contractors when the demand was there. As part of our standard practice, we reinvested profit back into the business whenever possible to help ensure its survival. It was not an overnight success. By 1997, the family business had expanded its reach over the previous forty years, changing our farming systems from dairy farming to sheep farming to cattle and then to crops, while at the same time gradually purchasing neighbouring land when it was ready to be sold. This expansion allowed us to build our economies of scale, critical to financial survival in the world of intensive agriculture, using the high-cost farming equipment across more land for better economic return. Buying more land also meant we were farming on a range of different soil types with varying water absorption capacity. This helped to reduce risk with the variable rainfall—sometimes too much rain for the heavy clay soil and sometimes too little for the light loamy soil. In addition to expanding our farming land, the cattle feedlot was established as one of Australia's first. Its founders, the grandfather and grandmother of our farming family, are heralded still today as pioneers in this new and exciting industry. We employed all the strategies that we could to help achieve success. Economic success was our focus ... at what cost we did not yet understand.

Running this sophisticated, model-farming business was a family under pressure, but you wouldn't have known it. The grandfather, who helped to pioneer the Australian cattle feedlot industry, became a leading figure in Australia in what is now the dominant method for fattening cattle across the western world. The grandmother still feels a connection with the land and an eye for cattle recognised by all who know her. The father, my husband, is university educated and was philosophically committed to growing food to help feed the world. He had a clear vision for his family's farming business, and he was dedicated to that vision for himself and for his family. He transformed its operation to this extraordinary model of efficiency, introducing technology and land-use practices that were considered by his peers and industry leaders to be leading edge and world class.

I am the mother in this farming family. I am university educated and have farming in my blood. For our children, every stem of their family tree includes farmers. Woven around bringing up our family, I threw myself into the business of modern agriculture both on our farm and on a larger scale, promoting the cleverness of agriculture to the broader Australian community. Our three children rode horses, motor bikes, and bicycles, swam in the house dam, and loved it when the floodplains filled with water so they could slide in the mud from the black soil and swim in the farm water drains.

But all was not well with our model farming family. That same grandfather had been bruised twice by failed business ventures trying to extend our farm supply chain. During these ventures, he felt the loss of control that comes with contracting your services to a multinational operation. The grandmother, who was so proud of her son as he transformed the farm into its model of efficiency, also felt her heart miss a beat every time she sacrificed a little more land where she grazed her small, precious herd of cattle on those open grasses. She accepted the sacrifice to make way for the profitable crops that had to be planted. The father, as he felt his own health decline, continued to drive his body beyond its natural resilience in pursuit of success. He also sensed a gnawing feeling in his stomach that the farm he was developing could not last. Our inheritance was under threat. Not our financial inheritance but the metaphorical inheritance passed down through all those branches in our children's family tree— the inheritance of farming, of connection, of growing food to feed the world. As the mother of our young children, I found myself watching on, powerless as I saw our children become isolated from the farm and from their father whose workload was incessant as he was so determined to build our business and at the same time protect our children from the chemical and machinery dangers that go hand in hand with this modern farming life.

So much was gained over those forty years, and yet so much was lost as well. Fast-forward another ten years to 2007. By this time, the wheels were in motion for our farm to be sold, ultimately to a public company, convinced that it could add value for its shareholders by including this model farm to a suite of land that made up its burgeoning agricultural enterprise. Just five years later, our farm was for sale again, having not delivered its promised treasures to those who keep giving less and demanding more.

How, you might ask, is our family's story relevant to man's changed position on Mother Earth?

It is relevant in so many ways.

At first glance, this fifty-year story appears as a microcosm of fifty years of industrial agriculture, reflecting the influence of modern scientific thinking and economic rationalism. It is that and much more as well.

This is a story of real lives playing out man's struggle with his place on earth.

A Dichotomy of Thinking

At the centre of this struggle is the philosophical question of whether we are separate from or part of the universe in which we live, whether humans are interconnected with that universe or whether we exist independently.

Such consideration highlights the difference between linear and holistic methods of thinking. Linear thinking aims for absolute measurement by breaking things down into their component parts in order to understand how they work, then applying this knowledge to achieve new or improved results by manipulating these parts, one variable at a time. By contrast, holism is the idea that a particular system cannot be explained by its component parts alone, and moreover that the whole is different from the sum of its parts. The linear methods of thinking are highly prized by our modern scientific community, allowing all things to be measured independently in order to prove their influence. The notion of holism is considered to be alternate thinking by many people in our western societies, surpassed by scientific approaches refined over the centuries since the ideas of Descartes, regarded by many as the father of modern philosophy. Descartes proposed a mechanistic framework for the operation of plant, animal, and human bodies, along with a dualistic distinction of the immaterial mind from the body.

At the extreme of this dichotomy of thinking is whether or not our minds influence our bodies and the world around us. Questions located more centrally on the spectrum are whether there could be a link between our modern agricultural systems and the chronic state of ill health sweeping the wealthy western nations of the world, and whether our modern methods of mechanically focused medical diagnosis and treatment may be missing the central notion of holism of the human body. Interwoven with these questions is whether our approach to the ecology of our landscape is central to the improvement in well being of humans on this planet.

From the knowledge available to us today, it seems that the answer is yes to these fundamental questions.

As the mother in this family, I have been asking myself versions of these questions, from our family's perspective, for more than twenty-five years. As our family's life journey helps us to find our own answers, we may find answers for others as well.

Today, we have left the farm and are healing the deep wounds that developed in those years. Not financial wounds. We managed that part well. If there's one thing we were all good at, it was the business of farming. Ours have been the wounds of emotional and physical health. Those that can be labelled include stroke, depression, chronic fatigue, a range of autoimmune conditions, and a string of emotional breakdowns. Through it all, we kept our heads high and soldiered on until we could no longer ignore the signs.

Our land, too, suffered its breakdowns. Not that you would have known it from the yields of our crops.

Each year, each new piece of technology, combined with a steel-like focus and discipline, helped us to get things right—helped us to stay ahead of the game. Breakdowns in humans eventually confront you, and they have to be dealt with. Breakdowns in the land are a little quieter. We don't hear the calls for help. On our farm, the technology we were using masked what was really happening. That technology kept giving us higher yields, but our land's natural productive capacity continued to diminish. Weeds and insects took more controlling. The quantity of fertiliser we needed to use kept increasing. Our land was sick too.

We made our choices with the knowledge that we had. We used all the intellect and analysis that we could muster.

Having ticked all the boxes that we could find to measure our success, we watched it slip through our fingers, and with it we participated in the last linkages of a family whose heritage, whose heart beat, was farming.

In our search, what did our family miss? What is modern man missing?

There's More to Life than Meets the Eye

In life, we only know what we know, and we don't know what we don't know. At an analytical level, that's true. At an intuitive level, that may not be so.

I think what we missed on our farm, and what the world is missing, is a question that sits above all that focus, all that analysis, and all those decision-making skills—a question that asks "What can nature provide?" What in nature's bounty are we missing? Might we be healthier as people if we tapped into some of these treasures? Might our land and food be healthier too if we listened more to nature's messages?

Gradually, as the father and the mother in our family, Bill and I were both drawn to the same conclusion but down different paths. We knew something was wrong; deep down, we knew it. At first, we didn't want to hear it. Bill's knowing was displayed by a deep anxiety expressing concern about our future. "This business model is not going to last. The land can't keep going. We are in the middle of all this." Eventually the realisation for Bill was that we would have to change our farming practices or otherwise stop farming. We chose the latter for lots of different reasons.

For me, it wasn't so clear. It was just that there was something fundamentally wrong with our choices at so many levels. I can see now that there were two parts to those choices that were gnawing away at me. Both were confronting in different ways. The first choice that we made was as farmers. Our family was living and working on a farm that had virtually been reduced to a wheat factory and a meat factory. There wasn't much that was natural happening on our farm. It was all about increasing control. Being part of that industrialised system for more than twenty years meant that we were constantly under emotional and physical pressure, as well as being exposed to a toxic array of chemicals. What effect was this having on our own health and on the health of our land?

In addition to being farmers, I was also the main purchaser of food for our family. This was gnawing away at me too. This is the type of choice that we all have to make as modern western consumers in the world. We buy our food from supermarkets and produce stores, sourced from all over the world and distributed to our local retail outlets. How healthy is that food if it has been grown and stored using these modern industrialised farming methods that I have been describing?

Our family represents a microcosm of these issues facing modern food production on the one hand and modern consumers on the other. Both hands are joined.

Metaphorically speaking, our family represents the heart of it all.

Without Rhyme or Reason

One of the characteristics that separate man from beast is our ability to reason. It has advanced mankind to extraordinary heights. As we have advanced our rational reasoning, one of nature's treasures that I think we have left behind is the power to harness our intuitive and instinctive reasoning.

Intuitively, instinctively, don't we recognise that something is radically wrong? Don't we sometimes wonder, just sometimes, whether apples stored for twelve months, treated and irradiated, then transported across the world before they are polished up and sold as "fresh" apples might actually be lacking in some fundamental goodness?

Intuitively, instinctively, didn't we as a family recognise that something was wrong with our "perfect" farming model? Didn't we recognise that by soaking our grain seeds in a chemical (to kill the ants that would otherwise hinder germination of the seed) might actually contaminate that plant in some way? We knew that the chemical was dangerous to us, and we took whatever protective measures we could when we were handling the chemical and the treated seeds. What we didn't do was join the dots. We buried our intuitive and instinctive reasoning (the reasoning that says "Hang on! What is really going on here?") and allowed our rational reasoning to dominate in order to achieve our identified goals, and supply grain to meet that world demand brought about by an ever-expanding population. What we were doing was meeting demand and working our hardest to achieve the best results possible. And we were good at it.

Intuition and instinct are available to us all free of charge. We just have to learn to tap into them again. That takes us beyond our five senses. How does our rational mind handle that gut feeling, that knowing? I don't think our family members are the only ones in the world who missed it. What could be possible in the choices we create if we were able to harness that energy to be part of our everyday life?

There are signs that man's awareness may be evolving to a new level. We may be embracing perceptions beyond our five senses, which previously limited our perspective as well as our analytical and decision-making abilities.

For me, energy is at the centre of this new understanding. Energy exists in many forms and at many different levels—from energy that is consciously harnessed by humans, such as the food we eat to fuel our bodies and the electricity we use to fuel our modern lives, to energy that is mostly not recognised and yet influences us greatly. This energy includes the earth's energy systems that change with the daily waxing and waning of the moon, and the energy that is generated by our individual conscious and subconscious thoughts. These latter forms of energy are largely disregarded by our measureable, tangible scientific world.

This book allows us to take a fresh look at understanding at least some of the power of that energy and its role in our levels of awareness. This book also explores how, with a dose of humility and a renewed respect for the extraordinary healing power of nature, we can tap into this energy to regain our own health and well-being and at the same time contribute, little by little, to healing our planet. It awakens the use of some ancient practices that contribute to the health of our landscapes, our animals, and ourselves by bringing these practices back to life and showing us how they are relevant in our modern world. Also, within the pages of this book, real food is rediscovered as a healing agent and a foundation to our health and well-being. Our thoughts, our consciousness, and our intuition are also explored as tools for our power to heal.

Is our modern civilisation in decline? That's a big question. There are signs of decline around us. There are also signs of great hope and possibility. Perhaps by starting from within, we create the best chance of expanding our understanding of our enormous power and capacity, and then to balance that power with our currently unfettered desire to dominate. By applying that power from within, we may instead find some new ways to work in harmony with planet Earth, on which, after all, we ultimately depend.

Chapter 2

Soils Ain't Soils

Let's first of all consider the most obvious form of energy connected with the life of our farming family—man's need for food and the source of that food, the earth. For us and many other farming families, helping to feed the world was a motivating part of our lives.

The transformation of the food systems of the western world since World War II has been chronicled by Michael Pollan in his book *The Omnivore's Dilemma*. Without realising it, that decision to convert the weapons factory in Alabama into a fertiliser factory in 1947, drew a line in the sand where modern reductionist science and economic rationalism became the central players in the decision-making frameworks for the western world. They infiltrated our families, our communities, and our national policies with mind-blowing speed and dominance. They are clear, simple, and measurable. No longer do we need to deal with the nebulous world of the unknown. We conduct the experiments and apply the results to a much anticipated and expected outcome.

No clearer or more powerful a story can be found to begin to demonstrate the impact of this newfound measurability and rationalism than the story of our soils, our food systems, and our own human health.

The first question to ask ourselves is how, despite our best intentions, we appear to have achieved a decline in the intrinsic state of human health in the western world. This is most starkly represented by the increases in chronic diseases in recent decades. At the top of the list are stroke, heart attack, arthritis, cancer, and diabetes.

Chronic Disease Statistics

AUSTRALIA	USA
• Chronic diseases are the primary health concerns for Australians	• 40% of the total USA population is affected by some form of chronic disease
• In 2010, cancer accounted for 3 out of 10 registered deaths in Australia	• 7 out of 10 deaths in the USA were due to chronic disease in 2009
• Diabetes prevalence more than doubled in the two decades leading up to 2005	• Multiple chronic diseases is now prevalent amongst older adults in the USA
• $1,500 million was spent on treating diabetes in Australia in 2008-2009	• Chronic diseases account for $3 of every $4 spent on health care in the USA

Illustration 1. Chronic disease statistics for
Australia and the United States.[1, 2, 3]

This is occurring at the same time as we venture forth with increasingly sophisticated medical discoveries, increased publicly funded health budgets, the adoption of advanced agricultural practices, and a clear commitment to the wonders of modern science and economic rationalism.

The Weapons Factory

The story behind the transformation of the weapons factory may provide us with a few of the answers. The two main protagonists in this story are a German chemist, Fritz Haber, and one of nature's heavyweights, the mighty mycorrhizal fungi, a largely invisible organism living in our soils. As Michael Pollan so deftly uncovered, it was the virtually unknown Fritz Haber who won the Nobel Prize in 1920 for "improving the standards of agriculture and the well-being of mankind."[1] He was heralded by some as providing one of the most important inventions of the twentieth century.

That invention was the chemical process required to manufacture synthetic nitrogen, the element in nature that is critical to life on earth. Prior to this invention, our plants relied on natural processes to provide them with that critical element, nitrogen, for healthy growth. These natural processes are limited in their uptake of nitrogen. Although nitrogen makes up much of the earth's atmosphere, most of this nitrogen is not naturally available for plant growth. Fritz Haber's invention meant these natural processes were no longer required, and nitrogen could be manufactured and added to the soil to enhance plant growth.

The perspective motivating the application of Haber's invention, as Pollan has written, came from the work of another German scientist more than half a century earlier. In 1840, Baron Justus von Liebig determined that there were only three elements in the soil that gave the plants their necessary nutrients. They were nitrogen, phosphorous, and potassium. Access to these three nutrients, according to Von Liebig, gave the plants all they needed for growth. Supplies of phosphorous and potassium are available to be mined from the earth. They can be transported and manufactured into a form that makes them available as an additive to the soil. It is the critical element, nitrogen, which required a chemical discovery to make it available for use beyond nature's cycles.

> *The link to the weapon's factory is that synthetic nitrogen was being used to make weapons. Once the war was over, that same synthetic nitrogen started to be used to make fertiliser.*

And so the mass transformation of our food supplies began. All three elements became routinely available as inorganic fertilisers bearing the letters from the scientific periodic table N-P-K.

The production of artificial fertilisers had begun in various forms in the previous century. It was the combination of the availability of cheap artificial fertiliser (through cheap fuel) and its use on the extremely responsive corn plant in the United States that tipped the scales to the large-scale uptake of artificial fertiliser applications.

Nitrogen's availability was the most significant of the three elements in the N-P-K combination because life on earth is dependent on adequate levels of accessible nitrogen. As Pollan points out, the quantity of nitrogen available for uptake by plants creates a ceiling to the quantity of life on earth, as nitrogen is the building block for all life.

A moment of reflection may draw you to consider the enormity of this discovery.

Could it be that the application of artificial fertilisers, used increasingly across the agricultural landscape since the 1940s, is the single greatest reason for the population explosion the earth has experienced in the past sixty years?

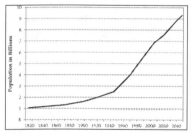

Illustration 2a. World population growth since 1820.[1]	Illustration 2b. World grain production since 1950.[5]

As can been seen from illustration 2a, the massive explosion in the world's population began around 1950. This paralleled the uptake of artificial fertiliser, allowing grain production, as shown in illustration 2b, to also increase in concert with world population.

Enter now the second of our protagonists, the 'mighty' mycorrhizal fungi. These fungi punch above their weight in every way. This discovery of a wonder of nature was made by another German scientist, Professor Albert Frank. His discovery occurred in 1885, almost midway between Liebig's N-P-K pronouncement in 1840 and Haber's invention of synthetic nitrogen in 1909. What began for Frank as an exploration into the possibilities of growing truffles in Prussia evolved into a theory of the symbiotic relationship between fungi and roots.

This theory turned conventional botanical wisdom on its head, but its promotion did not take hold. Instead, the western world embraced the application of Haber's invention of synthetic fertiliser. Now, more than a century later, the contrasts between nature's relationships and man's invention has finally come under the microscope.

Why the mycorrhizal fungi has never taken centre stage can possibly be explained by our preoccupation with modern science and its seemingly linear, reductionist approach. It would be an understatement to say that the relevance of the mycorrhizal fungi has taken a long time to be absorbed. By 2004, almost 120 years after Frank's discovery of this symbiotic relationship between the fungi and roots, it was noted by an American mycologist that "the conceptual revolution continues to this day, as the implications of mycorrhizal associations to evolutionary theory and plant ecology find their way slowly but inexorably into scientific thinking."[2]

So what are mycorrhizal fungi, and why should they be taking centre stage? Let's return to the natural cycle of plants and animals on earth to start to find the answer.

The sun provides our plants on earth with the energy to undertake the process of photosynthesis. Plants do this by taking carbon dioxide (CO_2) out of the atmosphere and returning oxygen (O_2) back into the atmosphere for animals to breathe. After animals breathe in the oxygen, they breathe out carbon dioxide, which then continues its cycle of absorption by the plant. This cycle explains what happens to the oxygen atoms (O_2) out of the carbon dioxide (CO_2). The other part, the carbon atom (C), puts the mycorrhizal fungi on centre stage. The plant takes the carbon down into its roots, and the magic begins. The symbiotic relationship identified by Frank more than a century ago occurs as a form of underground trading. The plant gives its carbon to the plant roots and to tiny little parasites living on the roots of the plant. The parasites, called fungal hyphae, are attached to the mycorrhizal fungi. In return for this liquid sugar (carbon energy), the fungi gift to the plant some minerals that have been absorbed from the soil and its living matter. This is a two-way trade. The mycorrhizal fungi are the middlemen in this silent deal. Without these fungi, the deal would not happen; soils would not receive carbon, and as a result, animals (including humans) would not receive the nutrients that we need for our health and well-being.

The clincher is that the plants only exchange the carbon for the nutrients if they need them for growth.

How, then, does Haber's synthetic fertiliser affect this story?

When plants are given water-soluble synthetic fertiliser, such as the N-P-K combination, to stimulate their basic growth needs, they no longer go searching for the wide range of minerals and nutrients that the soil can provide, and they no longer gift carbon to the soil. So the underground exchange stops. The cascading effect is enormous. It only starts to be recognised when we take it to the next stage and understand that our vitamins, minerals, and other nutrients are supplied to our body through the food that we eat, courtesy of the food chain over which we have come to preside. If the plants do not obtain these minerals from the soil, they will not be present in the plant, which means they will not be available to us in our food. In addition, when that plant stops searching for minerals for growth, as already mentioned, it also does not deliver the exchange of that atom of carbon into the soil. It is that carbon which allows the soil on earth to be replenished and rebuilt. The consequence, we ask?

> *The simple act of applying a synthetic fertiliser to speed up the growth of our plants could also be paving the way for the decay of human health through the decay of the soil that supports life on earth.*

Prior to 1947 when this story begins, Lady Eve Balfour, who founded the Soil Association in Britain, had already begun sounding the warning bells for this potential decline. In her book *The Living Soil*, she noted that the foods themselves, when still in a living state, showed a decline in resistance to ailments, described as "a lowered quality and vigour exactly parallel to that found in the human race."[3]

She also hinted at the potential long-term effects of this deterioration of foods and the corresponding human health, when expressing her own deep concerns about the direction of industrialised agriculture. "History suggests that a decline in soil fertility is always accompanied by a corresponding decline in the vigour of the people who dwell upon it."[4]

Perhaps Haber did make one of the most significant inventions of the twentieth century. Those of us who live in the twenty-first century may not be as generous in our recognition and praise. That decay is not immediate, of course. It happens over generations of animal offspring, including humans, and over decades of soil biological activity.

We will discuss later in the book that the compounding effect of malfunctioning cells can become too much for the body's immune system by the third generation in some animals and in some humans. We will also investigate later that our own awareness, understanding, and use of the power of our thoughts, along with a return to more traditional diets, play a pivotal role in changing the makeup of our cells to strengthen our immune system. We will see that our DNA does not determine our future; we do!

Building Blocks or Stumbling Blocks

Let's return now to nitrogen as the building block for life on earth. The newly created availability of this previously bound substance has provided us with new ammunition out of the same factory. The factory no longer uses nitrogen to make ammunition to try to dominate in active warfare against other human beings. It now uses nitrogen to make ammunition to try to dominate against nature and grow more food. We have been doing this with great success.

Our own farming family on the Darling Downs were active participants, supplying increased quantities of food on demand every year for fifty years, and the new owners are attempting to follow the same path. As the world's population has exploded, so too has the demand for food. This cycle continues with the increased food availability then supporting further increases in population. How long can this upward spiral keep going?

There is another energy resource demanded by our exploding world population. It, too, can be found in abundance in the same region Down Under on the Darling Downs, now used for farming. That resource is coal and natural gas, made available to modern man after millions of years of formation. There is a strange irony to the picture appearing here. To access the energy made from coal and natural gas, in order to provide clothing, shelter, and manufactured goods for the world's growing population, the farming land so prized for producing the world's food energy is now fighting for its very survival. We are witness to something that we have always laughed about when we have seen it in our family pets …

We are witness to man chasing his tail.

The ultimate irony is that some of this coal and gas is used to provide the energy that produces the fertiliser now being manufactured in our old ammunition factory and then applied to the crops on that same farming land! Who is laughing now?

Perhaps we are experiencing an overdose of linear thinking in our rush for economic growth to be the ultimate goal. Could it be that community prosperity, which implies a form of interdependence with the world around us, may be longer lasting and more meaningful as a goal for humanity? The economic growth model has dominated the decisions surrounding the transformation of our agricultural systems and mining activities. Now, combined with the conflict over land use to provide us with these essential sources of energy, this model threatens the long-term regenerative capacity of our landscapes to continue to support our ever-increasing demands.

Instead of creating our own building blocks for the future, have we created our own stumbling blocks?

As for the Soil, So for Our Bones

Earth is a living organism and part of the solar system, from which are generated the various forms of energy that support all life on the planet. In addition, the energy from all life on the planet helps to keep the structure of the earth intact. The cycle of growth involving decay and replacement is easily understood. The importance of this cycle to the regeneration of the earth and the impact of the interruption of this natural cycle is a little more difficult to absorb.

A world-renowned soils ecologist, Dr Christine Jones, is very outspoken on this issue. Some may say she takes a controversial stance. For the benefit of our future life on earth, this controversy may well be worthwhile. She holds strong views about how science is no longer serving the planet, no longer focusing on the observation of the natural process and asking "Why is that so?" but instead forsaking that observation for the manipulation of software programs to conduct its analysis and make its predictions. She says that our great scientists have been fabulous observers and that the prevailing approaches today are focused on whether or not a result fits a model … if not, there must be an error.

Dr Jones expounds the role of carbon in our soil. She parallels the carbon in our soils with the bones in the human body. The former is essential to the structure and ongoing health of the earth; the latter is essential to the structure and ongoing health of a person. And, she adds, they are also connected.

Here's how it works.

To maintain a healthy state, the soil and our bones are both constantly undergoing a process of decay and rebuilding. For the body, this is the death and replenishment of our cells. The human body takes from two days to replace the cells of our stomach lining to twenty-five years for the decay and replacement of all our bone cells. Osteoporosis literally means "porous bones," and the process begins when the body's bone cells are not replenished. For the soil, it takes from two days to two years for the soil to decompose. This means topsoil will also gradually disappear if it is not replenished. For both the bones and the soil, there are two parts to the process, decay and replacement. Decay happens anyway and is part of the natural process. It is replacement that is the key to longevity. This process of replacement is least understood and hence often disregarded. Our fertiliser factory comes back into the picture here, as does the mycorrhizal fungi—for both the soil and our bones.

As Dr Christine Jones points out, our soil requires both decomposition and replenishment to ensure its ongoing structure. Otherwise, the soil will gradually disappear. What was originally subsoil then becomes topsoil. We have already discussed how the carbon comes to the soil from the plant. The underground exchange that occurs between the mycorrhizal fungi and the soil roots allows the carbon to be retained in the soil and allows the minerals to be absorbed out of the soil. As Liebig identified, plants do not need this vast array of minerals for their growth. However, the world's food chain does require these minerals, and without the underground exchange, it does not happen. The soil also needs this exchange to occur so that the carbon atom (C) out of the CO_2 can make its way into the soil profile.

In the language of soil ecology, the dual processes of decay and replenishment involving carbon in the soil are called the decomposition pathway and sequestration pathway. Decomposition is the decay of the roots and plant matter to become organic matter in the soil. This organic matter combines with living organisms, and the minerals in the soil are created. Much of the carbon left in the soil from this process of decomposition is only temporary, lasting up to two years. It protects the soil and makes healthy topsoil, and it breaks down to feed the soil food web made up of fungi, bacteria, worms, and bugs. It can also disappear back into the atmosphere through soil disturbance, drought, or fire—hence its temporary status.

The second process, the sequestration pathway, is less understood. Sequestration adds extra carbon to the soil for its long-term structure and replenishment. Sequestration begins with photosynthesis, as already described, and ends with a stage called humification, which forms humus in the soil. This occurs continuously with the parasitic fungal hyphae dying every few days. The liquid carbon, which they have absorbed, is then eaten by another organism, which then dies, and the liquid carbon is released into the soil. Importantly, this process of making humus can only occur if there are fungal hyphae present, and fungal hyphae will only be present when the plant is seeking minerals for growth because this is when they are fed the liquid carbon from the plant.

Without humus, new soil is not formed, and the process of soil loss begins. Also, without humus, the first process of decomposition is much slower, as the humus provides life for the bugs and bacteria that assist with decomposition. In addition to the essential element of providing new soil through the sequestration pathway, the importance of the two pathways working in tandem provides extra life to the soil, which cannot be achieved otherwise.

Now to Our Bones

As already mentioned, our cells go through a constant process of dying and being replaced. Our bones take around twenty-five years to be totally replaced. Over each person's lifetime, every single cell in the body, including teeth, is replaced, often multiple times. We know our hair grows and falls out and in a healthy body is usually replaced; flaky skin is dead skin cells that have already been replaced. It is a little harder to visualise that the cells of our adult teeth are also completely replaced in our lifetime! Our bones form the physical framework on which our bodies hang. For our continued health, as the cells naturally die off, it is essential for new bone cells to be formed. Most cells form by splitting in half and growing again to form a new complete cell. The health of each cell is therefore critical to healthy production of new cells.

Minerals are an essential ingredient for that reproduction and growth to occur. There appears to be no definitive answer amongst the diverse medical fraternity as to how many macro and micro minerals our bodies need each day, but it is thought to be between forty-two and seventy-eight different minerals.[6] What is agreed is that we definitely need more than the three minerals, N-P-K, that were identified by Justus von Liebig for plant growth. Healthy growing plants draw the minerals out of the soil as long as there exists mycorrhizal fungi to exchange the carbon offered from the plant.

As Dr Jones points out, lack of minerals in the soil leads to lack of minerals in our foods, which ultimately leads to diseases in our civilisation.

Another gem that is drawn from certain plants when they are grown in healthy soils is the more recently understood nutrients known as glyconutrients. These glyconutrients combine with the minerals in the sap of the plant and give our bodies what Dr Nugent calls "the sugar code of life." They are the eight known monosaccharides, or simple sugars, that exist on the outside of every human cell in the form of glycoproteins. These glycoproteins provide the means for our cell-to-cell communication. Accurate communication requires an identical handshake between each cell to ensure the correct message is transmitted. Our immune system undertakes this cell-to-cell communication constantly. In a healthy body, the immune system's natural defence mechanism rids our bodies of unwanted free radicals that interfere with our cells' reproduction and growth. A healthy immune system with accurate cell-to-cell communication also destroys mutated cells. When this communication is not accurate, as can occur when a body is lacking sufficient nutrition, our body misreads cellular activity. The result is that it either allows free radicals and mutated cells to flourish, or it misfires and destroys the wrong cells. These two alternatives represent two probable health outcomes from an immune system that has been poorly functioning for an extended period. Mutated cells that survive can be cancer cells, and healthy cells that are destroyed by mistake, if this occurs often enough, can begin the onset of one or more autoimmune diseases. Such diseases in mild form include asthma and food intolerances. In more severe forms, they include multiple sclerosis, rheumatoid arthritis, and Type 1 diabetes.

That poorly functioning immune system can also affect the health and well-being of the next generation.

As already discussed, both these disease types, cancer and autoimmune conditions, have become increasingly prevalent in our wealthy western societies. Accurate cell-to-cell communication is critical to a well-functioning immune system and a healthy human being. In our modern diets, only two of these eight known simple sugars are generally present. Failure to obtain these glycoproteins in our diets means that our bodies must produce them, as they are essential to our cell-to-cell communication. Naturally enough, as our bodies come under pressure and can no longer produce sufficient glycoproteins, miscommunication starts to happen. As this miscommunication happens, disease can set in. As we continue to eat foods that are low in nutrient value, this pressure on our bodies also continues. The glycoproteins are then even more important and even less available, and so the cycle of ill health with a poorly functioning immune system can also escalate. These cells are the very same cells that are continuously produced to replace decayed cells in all parts of our body. As mentioned previously, critical to our well-being is the reproduction of healthy cells.

Parallel Lives

The parallels between our soil and our bones help to create a clear picture of the importance of the right food for both to ensure overall health. The food for our soil and the food for our bones come from the same process. This is called the carbon sequestration pathway. The energy from this pathway is the primary way that nature transfers carbon into the soil, allowing it continued renewal. It is also the primary way that nature transfers minerals and other nutrients out of the soil and into food, thus supplying us with the ability for continued cellular renewal. Without this pathway, driven by the mighty mycorrhizal fungi and the intricate web that is created, both the earth and humans suffer.

> *From this connection, it becomes apparent that we truly are dependent on our soils.*

It would have made life on earth very easy for modern man if only the N-P-K solution held true. Alas, not to be. Even in these few pages, the unravelling we are going through is becoming increasingly clear. There are, however, modern farming practices that do work with nature's cycles and are now being implemented by farmers who are seeking to reconnect with the natural energy available in these cycles. Later in this book, we look at some of these farming systems.

> *Armed with this new information, pieced together over almost a decade—of parallel lives between our soils and our bones, of missing links in our immune systems' communication, of the destructive role of artificial fertiliser denying fungi its ability to conduct its powerful exchange—so much that was previously so confusing has become a whole lot clearer to me.*

On our farm and many other farms like it, as the quality of our soil declined, we kept adding more artificial fertiliser to allow us to keep producing our crops. We didn't realise that adding this fertiliser was in fact making the situation worse, denying the soil its essential carbon atoms for renewal and denying the plants their essential minerals from that soil. Decay of the soils was definitely occurring as a natural process, but sequestration, which promotes replacement of soils, was not possible.

Plants definitely grow with the addition of a range of artificial fertilisers, including N-P-K, but what of their nutritional characteristics? We will see that fruits and vegetables are well documented as having lost the majority of their minerals and vitamins with the introduction of our industrialised farming systems. More on that later.

Chapter 3

The Animal and Plant Divide

One of the other characteristics of industrial agriculture, apart from the prevalence of artificial fertilisers, is that plants and animals no longer inhabit the same landscape. Animals can no longer select from a diverse range of pastures as they graze across the paddock. They are now fattened in feedlots similar to the one owned by our Darling Downs farming family, fed a strict regime of grains designed to provide the highest weight gain in the shortest time frame, with the most consistent meat characteristics possible.

How did we end up in this artificial, almost manufactured situation where we take the animals off the pastures and place them in a feedlot? What makes farmers choose to remove all the native pastures from their paddocks and plant a single crop that they then feed to the cattle in the feedlot? Add to these questions our knowledge that the digestive system of cattle is designed to eat grasses and is not designed to eat grains. Does this seem just a little absurd?

It is partially because of access to artificial fertilisers that this situation of plant and animal divide now exists.

Michael Pollan's investigation paints a fascinating picture of the analysis and decision making that drove the western world, including our farming family, to the current situation where plants and animals no longer inhabit the same landscape. The impact of this separation of nature's cycle also adds an important dimension to understanding the picture of where we find ourselves today.

By the 1940s, as the world was recovering from the ravages of two world wars in three decades, there appeared to be endless supplies of cheap oil. This was perfect for the increased production of nitrogenous fertiliser in factories similar to the old weapons factory, using Haber's recently discovered formula. Pollan has identified that it was this nitrogen fertiliser, when applied to the humble corn plant, that was at the centre of a complete rethink of the business of agriculture. Once this fertiliser was applied to the cornfields in the American Midwest, it became apparent that the potential increases in yield could provide not only food security but an economic boom to the United States. This new idea was so embraced that government policy shifted to promote the growing of corn as the most profitable activity for farmers ahead of all other crops.

And so the separation of the plants and animals began. From that point, it was only a matter of time before farmers responded to the financial carrot dangled in front of them. Worldwide, farmers are recognised as an extraordinarily adaptable and resilient group of people. Despite trying to control it, they still work with nature every day, so perhaps that makes them so. (This is not a throwaway line. In a later chapter, we will investigate the notion that our environment and our thoughts impact directly on our cellular makeup, so farmers' adaptability may indeed be because of their environment; having "farming in your blood" may be not so far from the truth.)

These farmers soon realised that they could earn a greater return from their farm if they grew corn on the land and fed it to their cattle after harvest. With the promise of increased yields simply by applying more fertiliser, (along with government subsidy to ensure a higher income), this option would provide a much better return than maintaining a complex mix of plant species growing at different times throughout the year and having to be managed in conjunction with the animals that graze the landscape. From this beginning came the development of the separate cattle feedlot industry. Some farmers then ceased to own cattle at all. They then became croppers specialising in the production of high-yield corn crops that they sold to other farmers who had become "feedlotters," specialising in feeding and fattening cattle on a mass scale in large, fenced enclosures devoid of any natural pastures.

This specialisation of occupation allowed for a more focused approach to each business, maximising resources for the highest possible economic return. It was encouraged and rewarded, with farmers seen to be entering the age of now running businesses where inputs and outputs could be accurately measured, allowing changes to be made to the systems that were implemented in order to improve the bottom line.

The acclaimed documentary movie, *Food, Inc.*, nominated for an Academy Award in 2010, adds another dimension to the momentum behind this shift in agricultural practice. Food, Inc. highlights the consumer's demand for a more consistent food product. It draws on the expansion of the fast-food phenomenon, focusing on one of the earliest and most successfully branded franchises, McDonalds. These fast-food chains are large purchasers of beef and other foods. A cornerstone of their businesses is that consumers can expect the same quality product no matter which store they purchase from. This demand played into the hands of the newly separated plant and animal industries. The feedlotters could design a specific ration of grain for their cattle to ensure that the right meat characteristics were developed to provide a consistent product to the market. As luck would have it, a diet of corn was found to provide the fastest weight gain in the cattle, so the croppers were very happy to supply their high-yielding corn that was being grown fence to fence and being encouraged by government policies.

For a short period, it seemed this would provide a fairy-tale ending for all involved. These newly developed, efficient models of production made their way across the oceans and were quickly adopted by farmers across the western world, including our farming family who successfully ran two businesses as both croppers and feedlotters, dovetailing each into the other.

Eventually this cycle will have to change. In addition to the obvious questions we need to ask about our human health, patterns are emerging now in the farming areas where industrial agriculture has dominated for more than half a century, showing that the demand for artificial fertilisers to maintain fertility, as well as chemicals to manage the weeds and insects, is consistently rising. Our farm was one such example. Even though the economic rationalist is still in charge and the inputs keep being added to try to boost production, that same economic rationalist is starting to think of different ways to feed the world.

He has to, because his singular focused model of "dominate nature, and you'll profit more" is now coming unstuck, with profit, productivity, and fertility all diminishing.

In the case of our family's farming business, that gut feeling, which was alluded to in the introduction to this book, finally identified itself as an awareness that the success we had experienced had also created an imbalance, both for our own health and for our farm's health. It also became clear that this imbalance could not continue.

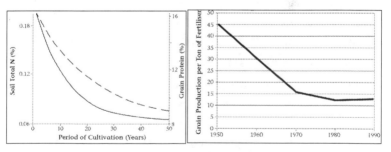

Illustration 3a. Decline in soil nitrogen and grain protein over fifty years (from 1940 to 1990).[6]

Illustration 3b. Decline in grain production per ton of fertiliser used (from 1950 to 1990).[5]

As shown in the graph in illustration 3a, as far back as 1990 it was widely publicised that farming land that had been continuously cropped for fifty years had lost virtually all of its natural nitrogen in the soil. At the same time, protein levels in the grain crops had reduced from 16 per cent to 9 per cent in that time.

Running in parallel with this decline in soil fertility and grain protein was the reduction in grain produced with each ton of fertiliser used. As the soil fertility declined, artificial fertiliser use increased to boost production, but there was still a declining result.

This is a stark example of the impact of artificial fertilisers such as N-P-K replacing the underground work of the mycorrhizal fungi. Within half a century (two or three generations), the decay in the soil and the nutritional value of wheat is obvious. Within that same half century, the decay in human health is also obvious. Perhaps this is not a coincidence?

If you have followed this story so far, you will no doubt be starting to recognise that our mighty mycorrhizal fungi has been well and truly left behind in the gold rush of agribusiness, as it has come to be known. This change in name is in itself cause for reflection. Now driven by the reasoning of linear science and economic rationalism, and dominated worldwide by conglomerates and public companies, we have curiously left behind the *culture* in agriculture. Our family has felt this shift first-hand, as have many like us. Although individually not able to quantify it, the populations of the western countries, as well as those countries moving to this social and economic model of agribusiness, continue to feel this shift at an exponential rate. Its evidence is in our state of soil health as well as our human health and the challenges the medical system is facing to reverse the trend.

As we become more aware of the fallibility of these momentous decisions surrounding the source of our food and our relationship with nature, we are shifting our focus to ways to restore nutrient-dense foods to the western diet.

The Weston A Price foundation is a modern pioneer in the promotion of recommendations surrounding traditional foods. The basis for the organisation's momentum came from the work of its namesake, a dentist from Ohio, Dr Weston A Price. Dr Price spent time each year over a decade travelling to different countries in the early twentieth century, studying the health of populations untouched by western civilisation. When Dr Price analysed the foods used by isolated peoples, he found that, compared with the American diet of that time, these foods provided at least four times the water-soluble vitamins, calcium, and other minerals, and at least ten times the fat-soluble vitamins from animal foods, including butter, eggs, and animal fats. Today's nutritional data from countries such as the United States, Britain, and Australia show that the decline in the level of vitamins and minerals in foods has fallen even further since Dr Price's initial research, down between 10 per cent and 100 per cent, with some foods no longer containing the vitamins and minerals that used to be present. The results in these diagrams are from research conducted on fruit and vegetables grown in the United Kingdom.

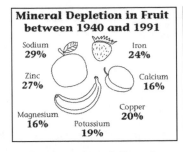

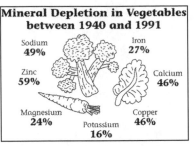

Illustration 4a. Mineral depletion in fruits from 1940 to 1991.[7, 8]

Illustration 4b. Mineral depletion in vegetables from 1940 to 1991.[7, 8]

The Weston A Price Foundation believes that much of this decline is due not only to the decline in soil health as already discussed but other key issues as well. One such issue surrounding decisions about our diet can be traced to another recent phenomenon we have already discussed, the separation of plants and animals from the same landscape.

Should Meat Be on the Menu?

This is a modern conundrum wrestled with by many families. We grew up with meat as a staple in our families' diets, and today we are being told meat is on the list for limited consumption, and even then only lean meat with a minimum of fat. To Dr Price, the fats provided by traditional meats are not only healthy for us but essential to allow the absorption of critical fat-soluble vitamins, such as A, D, and K_2. In addition, he argued that they also give our cell walls and membranes the stiffness they need to avoid damage, and they protect our heart, kidney, and liver. In contrast to our current diet dictum, the Weston A Price Foundation sees it this way. "Human beings have been consuming saturated fats from animal products, milk products and the tropical oils for thousands of years; it is the advent of modern processed vegetable oil that is associated with the epidemic of modern degenerative disease, not the consumption of saturated fats." [5]

So what would drive us to change so radically the list of foods that are suddenly no good for us? Our recently developed predisposition to linear thinking may have contributed. The Weston A Price Foundation provides an example by likening our modern obsession to reduce cholesterol (a major argument for reducing meat consumption and other saturated fats) to an act of shooting the messenger. The Foundation argues that because there is often higher than normal levels of cholesterol present after a heart attack, we have developed the logic that the cholesterol caused the heart attack. To the Weston A Price Foundation, nothing could be further from the truth. It argues cholesterol is present when the heart attack occurs because cholesterol is one of the body's natural healers. Blaming coronary heart disease on cholesterol is like blaming the firemen because they are always present when there is a fire. "Cholesterol is not the cause of heart disease but rather a potent antioxidant weapon against free radicals in the blood, and a repair substance that helps heal arterial damage." [6]

It seems almost absurd that modern medicine on the one hand and modern, traditional nutritionists on the other hand have such opposing views to the issue of diet— when everybody agrees that our diet is a critical element to our health. Our methods of logic and reasoning and our definition of science may help to explain this conundrum. We will return to this shortly.

Grass or Grain?

There is no argument that one characteristic of modern saturated fats is very different from those consumed by my grandparents' generation. As already identified, most meat consumed in western societies today comes from cattle fed on grain rather than cattle fed on grass. That change in diet to grain-fed meat creates a significant change in one of the characteristic of saturated fats. It seems common sense that the characteristics of a particular food could change based on what that food itself has eaten, although it is possibly unpalatable for modern agribusiness to digest. As consumers, we may find the consistent quality and flavour of grain-fed meat to be favourable, but the impact on our long-term health may not be.

Central to the difference in the fat qualities of meat from grain-fed cattle compared with grass-fed cattle is the change in ratio of omega-3 and omega-6 fatty acids. Omega-3, which has anti-inflammatory qualities when consumed, is largely found in grasses. Omega-6 has inflammatory qualities and is mainly found in grains. The Weston A Price Foundation says that traditional diets contain nearly equal amounts of omega-6 and omega-3 fatty acids. Meat from these traditional diets came from animals fed on grasses and not grains. Meat in our modern diets mainly comes from animals fed the exact opposite, grains and not grasses. It is well recognised that inflammation is a central characteristic in modern diseases such as heart disease, diabetes, and cancer. The ratio of traditional diets of 1:1 for their consumption of omega-6 to omega-3 fatty acids contrasts dramatically with today's consumption of beef, chicken, and eggs that are mainly fed on grain rather than grass. This imbalance of omega-6 to omega-3 can now be as high as 19:1.

This issue identifies another unforeseen consequence of our decision to separate our plants and animals from the same landscape. When they were together, the natural cycle of the plants being consumed by the animals, and then the animals being consumed by humans, meant the meat we ate was far more balanced than the semi-manufactured meat, chicken, and eggs available today. Grass has been replaced by grain ... and we are feeling the consequences ... and so the effects of our linear, industrialised world continue to flow on.

> *As I came to understand the difference between the nutritional qualities of meat from cattle that have been fed on grain compared with cattle that have been fed on grass, it was almost like taking a bullet for our family.*

I saw the enormous flaw in our previous practice, and I wondered whether I could ever voice this new information without threatening the proud identity of three generations. We pioneered the industry that feeds grain to cattle, the cattle feedlot industry. We staked our family's future on the success of that industry based on the research that the world's population was continuing to grow and that increased prosperity would create increased demand for meat as a major source of protein. Grain-fed meat would satisfy that demand. We fed our own grain-fed meat to our own children without a moment of hesitation, confident in the knowledge that meat provides many essential nutrients.

> *We didn't realise that this meat, grain-fed meat, wasn't really meat as our bodies had been used to. It was something rather different, having been fed grain and not grass.*

Banish the Bugs

Another part of the plant and animal divide is the increased need for pesticides and herbicides that have arisen since the plants and animals have been separated from the same landscape. As seems only natural, when they coexisted, animal numbers were limited by food supply, and their interdependence provided the natural cycle of management of all plants and insects in the ecosystem. Once they were separated, the natural cycle was broken, and artificial controls became essential to stop rampant disease and to provide certainty of product to market. The result for modern consumers is the prevalence of chemicals now in our food chain.

Our practices on our farm were no different from this description. We needed more and more chemicals to control more and more pests, both weeds and insects, as the years progressed. We followed all the standards laid down for application rates and waiting periods between spraying the pests and harvesting the crops. Australia's requirements are high by world standards. We can't be certain whether Bill absorbed toxins from the farm over all those years. He knows though, intuitively, instinctively … more about that later too.

These explanations are not given to specifically highlight the importance of the right ratio of fats in our diet or to highlight any particular chemical. They are given to help demonstrate the consequences of our decisions when we attempt to dominate nature, of which we are an integral part … ultimately, we feel the consequences of our own domination.

So how did I share all this confronting information with our family?

I started writing, privately, trying to put into context what I was learning. Once I had written enough, I shared my written words with our family, all three generations. Having read it, I asked them whether they were comfortable for me to continue writing and maybe making it public one day. Their support was unconditional. In the end, we all realise that we make our choices based on what we know. We learn throughout life, and we adjust and adapt as we gain new knowledge.

Today, in our family, we make very different choices about our food and our nutrition. The food on our table doesn't look much different. What is different is its origins and how it is prepared. We believe that we are consuming food closer to the natural source and resembling the more traditional diets of our ancestors. We believe that is better for all of us.

What Now?

There are alternative farming practices known to us that tap into natural energies generated by the plant and animal interaction with the soil, tapping into the power of the mycorrhizal fungi. They do this, in part, by keeping the plants and animals on the same landscape. These are old practices, reinvented for modern times. In some parts of the world, they have never died out. How the farmers manage the interaction between the plants, animals, and the soil determines how healthy and productive this landscape can be. As we now see, it also determines the density of the nutrition of the foods grown on this landscape.

Littered around the world in the western countries that pursue these industrialised agricultural systems, there is a groundswell of people who have taken up the challenge of developing and implementing alternative options to this industrial farming model. A range of natural farming systems are now flourishing and tapping into many aspects of modern technology. One such transformation has been quietly occurring in Australia for more than twenty-five years, headed by an educator by the name of Dr Terry McCosker.

Dr Terry McCosker's search for ecologically balanced farming systems led him to the work of a naturalist from Rhodesia (now Zimbabwe) by the name of Allan Savoury. Based on his observations of the herd movements of African game animals, Savoury developed principles for modern grazing systems that mirror those herd movements, with intense activity on the landscape from a large mob for a short period of time—several days at the most.

It may seem counterintuitive—large mobs of livestock actually re-vegetating the landscape ... really? Yes, really. Timing is critical. Large herds excrete and urinate over their own food, and in nature they keep moving. Moving on in a short period of time prevents the overgrazing of plants. The short-term, aggressive trampling process ensures good coverage of the soil with fresh seeds, natural fertilisers, and mulch from the trampled grass. Gradually, undernourished, and sparsely covered landscapes rebuild to productive soils with lush pastures. Once re-established, these landscapes are then totally re-engaged with the mycorrhizal fungi, and the rich natural cycle of plant and animal life can flourish.

In the modern farming environment, this process is managed to ensure that the animals are not moved onto the landscape until the plants have reached a phase of growth where the natural sugars are at their highest and most nutritious. Once this fresh growth has been eaten and the critically important trampling process has occurred, the mobs are then moved on to another paddock of native grasses that are at the correct phase of growth to be eaten.

Dr McCosker is now one of the world's most acknowledged champions of holistic farming practices, with a twenty-five-year history as an educator, an unparalleled reputation of technical farming knowledge in this field, a refusal to accept a linear reductionist approach to nature, and a client base of farmers across Australia and South Africa—taking the message back to the doorsteps of where it all began with Allan Savoury's observations. Dr McCosker is supported around Australia and in South Africa by many practitioners who have become educators themselves, sharing the principles and their own rich experiences.

I have spent ten years working alongside Terry McCosker and his Australian educators and practitioners, marvelling at their knowledge and commitment, thinking differently, and contributing fiercely to the future of the world's healthy food systems. It is through this network of farmers and educators that I came to understand the work of Dr Christine Jones and her graphic explanation of the parallels between our soils and our bones.

Dr McCosker is also fond of quoting another great naturalist, Sir Albert Howard, who was a botanist and is recognised as being the founder of the modern organic movement. Howard's most famous work, *An Agricultural Testament*, was first published in 1940. In the introduction to this book, Howard states that the main principles underlying nature's agriculture can be seen most easily in our woods and forests. "Mixed farming is the rule: plants are always found with animals: many species of plants and of animals all live together. In the forest every form of animal life, from mammals to the simplest invertebrates, occurs. The vegetable kingdom exhibits a similar range: there is never any attempt at monoculture: mixed crops and mixed farming are the rule ... In this way the soil is always protected from the sun, wind and rain ... The rain is also carefully conserved by its gradual absorption into the well structured soil ... The forest manures itself by making its own humus and supplies itself with minerals ... The mineral matter needed by the trees and the undergrowth is obtained from the subsoil."[7]

I am familiar with two other forms of natural farming systems that are gaining interest and uptake around the western world. They are permaculture and biodynamic agriculture. I have only started to learn about these two natural farming methods in the past five years. My personal knowledge is limited, but I am encouraged by what I have learnt through occasional lectures, field days, farm visits, conversations, and reading. I believe they will both increase in practice in coming years because they both tap into nature's cycles, allowing the replenishment of carbon and humus to our soils, thus supporting the activities of the mycorrhizal fungi and allowing them to flourish.

Permaculture acknowledges the role of humans in the ecosystem and consciously attempts to minimize the human footprint. It was conceived in Australia in the 1970s by Bill Mollison and David Holmgren and has since been taken up by many educators and practitioners, one of whom is Geoff Lawton. Geoff Lawton has established the Permaculture Research Institute, focused on the education and farm scale demonstration of permaculture principles. The emphasis in permaculture is on "consciously designing landscapes which mimic the patterns and relationships found in nature ..."[8] It uses zones to organise design elements in a human environment on the basis of the frequency of human use and plant or animal needs. The uptake of permaculture is most common for smaller scale food production, although its production capacity far exceeds other small-scale models due to the actual design features. As we return to more local production models of food supply in an effort to rebuild the nutritional density of our foods, I believe permaculture will become a very effective model to use.

Biodynamic agriculture is based on the work of Austrian philosopher and scientist Rudolf Steiner. It is drawn from a series of eight lectures that he gave in 1924. Biodynamic farmers conduct their farming activities not only in sync with the soil and its water and mineral cycles but also in sync with the etheric powers of the universe. They conduct their farming activities following the moon's cycles, based on the view that the moon governs the earth's growth and fertility cycles. According to the discipline of biodynamics, "Conclusions about the whole are based on observing the living plant in rhythmic time and seeing, with the mind's eye, the plants' essential 'Beingness.'"[9] Field applications used to enhance the soil and plant health are stored and prepared in ways that resonate with the energies of the earth and the sun. Perhaps not surprisingly, one of the essential principles of biodynamics is "Behind all matter and forces (i.e., everything) is the activity of Spirit."[9] Biodynamic foods are increasingly becoming available in specialised food outlets in western societies.

Einstein is often quoted as saying, "We cannot solve our problems with the same thinking we used when we created them." In our family's situation, we realised that the long-term health and productivity of our farm required a new set of paradigms to keep feeding the world. Although we had been operating with the best of intentions, no longer was it effective or appropriate for us to work within the mind-set of industrial agriculture, maintaining a mechanistic perspective to the production of food from our farm. It is clear that we are not alone in that realisation.

What set of paradigms do we need now? If we are so dependent on the earth, are we really separate from it? Before we explore this question, I have more to share about the body's power to heal—naturally.

As a family, our journey with food continues. We are constantly exploring and adapting as we uncover more information and take on changes to our own food preparation and consumption.

> *These days, our meat and eggs are grass fed. That's an easy sentence to write, but it was a massive change to make in our lives.*

We are fortunate to live where organic produce is readily available. We have also taken up the traditional practice of fermentation to support the healing power of good food and boost our bodies' healing processes.

That's not the whole answer though to our healing story. Our exploration continues. Once we began this questioning process in search of clues to return ourselves to an improved state of health, we found that all sorts of possibilities started to reveal themselves to us.

Chapter 4

Am I Stuck with the Genes I Inherited?

"When Science turned away from Spirit, its mission dramatically changed. Instead of trying to understand the 'natural order' so that human beings can live in harmony with that order, modern science embarked on a goal of control and domination of nature."[17]

According to Dr Bruce Lipton, the science of epigenetics profoundly changes our understanding of how life is controlled. "In the last decade, epigenetics research has established that DNA blueprints passed down through genes are not set in concrete at birth. Genes are not destiny! Environmental influences, including nutrition, stress, and emotions, can modify how these genes behave without changing their basic blueprint. And those modifications, epigeneticists have discovered, can be passed on to future generations as surely as DNA blueprints are passed down via the double helix."[18]

Once again, from yet another perspective, we are seeing that our own body is a complex system that responds to the world around it. In simple terms, DNA represents the cell's long-term memory, passed from generation to generation. RNA is a short-term replica.

The RNA functions as the active memory that is used by the cell as a physical template in synthesizing the proteins, which are the molecular building blocks that provide for the cell's structure and behaviour. Because the character of a living organism is defined by the nature of its proteins and its proteins are encoded in the DNA, it had previously been assumed "that the DNA would represent the 'first cause,' or primary determinant of an organism's traits."[19]

However, the more recent study of epigenetics sees it differently. Lipton defines epigenetics as control "above genetics," taking the Latin root epi which means upon or over. An operational definition attempted by a group of scientists in 2009 reads" "An epigenetic trait is a stably heritable phenotype resulting from changes in a chromosome without alterations in the DNA sequence."[20] Whether you are comfortable with the layman's explanation or the scientists definition, it is has been agreed in recent years through the study of epigenetics, that environmental influences affect cell behaviour, including its reproductive ability.

As Cyndi Dale explains it, "Epigenetics is the study of epigenomes, certain chemicals and switches that instruct the genes." She goes on to say that epigenomes "respond to alterations in the environment and then 'toggle' the DNA. Epigenetic changes often occur during DNA transcription, when the DNA is being copied."[21]

What we inherit from our ancestors is not entirely a predetermined genetic makeup. The science of epigenetics has made it clear that there are two mechanisms by which organisms pass on hereditary information. Those two mechanisms provide a way for scientists to study both the contribution of nature (genes) and the contribution of nurture (epigenetic mechanisms) in human behaviour. To Dr Bruce Lipton, "If you only focus on the blueprints, as scientists have been doing for decades, the influence of the environment is impossible to fathom."[22]

According to Lipton, the long-held view that our genes determine our destiny has now been challenged. Genetic determinism argues that it is a one-way flow starting with our DNA influencing our RNA, which determines the protein formation in our cells, which then influences a cell's structure and behaviour. Not so, according to Dr Lipton.

He says that the story of epigenetic control is the story of how environmental signals, not our DNA, control the activity of our genes. So what is environment? All those things that we intuitively know affect our well-being are what constitute our environment. Air, water, and physical exercise are environmental factors that are commonly recognised as impacting our health. Food is under the microscope here, and we will also take a much deeper look at the power of our thoughts in coming chapters.

All these factors influence our individual well-being, the health of our cells, and the messages passed back through the RNA to the DNA and to another level of proteins called regulatory proteins. According to Lipton, it is these regulatory proteins that respond to the environmental signals and help to demonstrate that the flow of information is not unidirectional from the DNA to the cell. It is these environmental signals that Cyndi Dale refers to when she notes, "Epigenetics suggests that social and emotional events can be chemically programmed into non-DNA substances, which in turn influence DNA activity. These events are passed down inter-generationally."[23]

Again, we have a two-way trade or a symbiotic relationship taking place in our bodies and influencing our health and well-being. Our body is constantly adapting to the world around it.

> *Epigenetics shows us that how we think and what we eat not only influence our own well-being but ultimately the well-being of our offspring and their offspring to follow!*

So when does the environmental influence begin, and for how many generations does it carry on? In short, it begins straightaway and continues to evolve as other influences occur in our lives.

> *Making the best possible choices for any situation is not only in your own best interest but also the best interest of your descendants.*

Pottenger's Cats

For ten years, between 1932 and 1942, Dr Frank Pottenger Jnr conducted a not-since-repeated study on the effects of nutrition on cats. What he discovered helps to shed some light on the power of epigenetics.

Five groups of cats were fed five different diets. What was considered an adequate diet was fed to the control group. This was a cat's normal food of raw meat scraps and raw milk, with the addition of cod liver oil. The other four groups were fed a different combination of meat and milk, with increasing quantities of cooked and processed meat and milk in each group. The final group was fed only a metabolised Vitamin D milk.

The study was conducted over four generations of cats, and the findings included the results for more than nine hundred cats. The findings detail the physical and emotional problems that developed in the animals fed the denatured and processed foods compared with the raw meats and milk that cats traditionally eat.

Four generations later, the control group, which was eating a traditional diet for cats, was flourishing with good reproductive health, thick and healthy coats, good dental health, unaltered facial and body structure, no social anxiety or depression, and no food allergies.

By contrast, all of the other groups developed to varying degrees a range of structural deformities, social stress, allergies, tumours, heart issues and blood sugar issues with groups three to five showing the most obvious decline with a clear pattern developing. The first generation developed diseases or issues at the end of their lives. The second generation developed diseases in the middle of their lives. The third generation all developed diseases early in life, often at birth. Many died within the first six months. Others were unable to reproduce. Group five was least healthy and did not survive beyond three generations.

As part of the pattern of social anxiety issues, female cats became aggressive while the males became docile.

After just three generations, young animals died before reaching adulthood, and reproduction ceased.

This research conducted by Dr Pottenger in the 1930s correlates with many of the findings of Dr Weston A Price in the same time period when peoples from still recognised traditional cultures were consuming increasing quantities of processed foods. Structural body changes, reproductive difficulties, and emotional instability were the three main characteristics of Pottenger's multigenerational study. Today it is interesting to note the increasing prevalence of fertility clinics in our western societies, catering to both men and women. At the same time, eating disorders continue to increase, with consequential physical and emotional difficulties. In 2014 in Australia alone, it has been reported that there are almost one million people with eating disorders. This represents 4 per cent of the population. Both these patterns identified by the third and fourth generations of cats, social anxiety and difficulty reproducing, are prevalent in our modern societies.

Has it only taken four generations? Has the deterioration gradually increased with each subsequent generation? Modern industrialised agriculture started to take hold after World War Two, from the 1940s. That's three or four generations. Only by looking back into one's own family history can any individual answer this question. When considering the prevalence of chronic diseases, eating disorders, and mental conditions in our modern western societies, it seems as whole societies we are following this same trend.

So how does this fit in with the study of epigenetics and the notion that our environment influences our genes? It is widely accepted that family traits, such as personality characteristics, body structure, and facial features, to name but a few, are genetically influenced. Assumptions that such gene traits are impenetrable and not influenced by our environment is clearly challenged by these changes to body function, body structure, and emotional stability. When those traits start to change, what is causing the change? Dr Pottenger's study of cats and Dr Price's study of human groups both gave similar results. As generations were persistently exposed to processed foods of poor nutritional quality, the social and structural changes became more obvious.

> *Dr Pottenger's study of cats was a controlled experiment that ceased after ten years. The deterioration in humans that Dr Price identified appears to be continuing to this day.*

According to Bruce Lipton, changes in nutrition and the cell's responses to those changes are environmental signals that feed into the DNA to then change the structure and behaviour of those cells without changing the actual blueprint. The health and characteristics of a particular cell influences the health and characteristics of the subsequent cells that are duplicated from it.

Dr Lipton also believes that the influence of our thoughts on our DNA is equally as important as the impact of our food, air, and water. This leads us to the next part of this story—the power of our thoughts.

Chapter 5

Are Our Thoughts the Real Placebo?

Food is not the only healing agent. So, too, are our thoughts.

Molecules of Emotion

Our thoughts are an integral part of our environment. Thoughts generate emotions, and emotions generate thoughts. Emotions are connected to our heart. Our heart not only pumps blood. It also makes the molecules of emotion. What does that mean?

A person's emotional state and the level of coherent function of various parts of the body are demonstrated when we study the production of chemicals in our body. It appears that every change in the mental-emotional state causes a change in the body's physiology. Similarly, every change in the body's physiology also causes a change in the mental-emotional state. Dr Candace Pert's discovery of neuropeptides in the 1970s provided some tangible explanation for what we already knew—sometimes our bodies respond to our emotions, and sometimes our emotions are generated in response to a physiological change. Frequently, these responses seem to be virtually instantaneous. No matter which way it goes, this provides an undeniable link between our minds and our bodies and a seemingly obvious connection between our emotional and physical well-being.

Neuropeptides are the key to this particular two-way trade. Examples of these protein molecules are dopamine, serotonin, and oxytocin—chemicals associated with happiness, security, and sense of worth. Our thoughts and emotions activate our body to produce these chemicals, and the very existence of these chemicals in our bodies makes it easier for us to maintain these thoughts and emotions.

The hundreds of neuropeptides are produced in the brain and the heart and throughout the body. This neuropeptide information is then exchanged through all systems of the body. So our heart not only pumps blood it also produces the molecules of emotion.

For Deepak Chopra, this constant flow of information and chemical exchange means that the heart is chemically and structurally a different organ each time it responds to a different emotion, such as a sense of loss compared with a feeling of sincere love. He believes that the heart is a different organ in different states of consciousness.

Examples of physiological responses to our thoughts and emotions have been recorded in many different ways.

Norman Cousins' autobiographical account of his recovery from an "incurable" illness provides the reader with some most insightful findings. Titled *Anatomy of an Illness as perceived by the Patient,* the introduction to Cousins' book is written by the French/American microbiologist, Emeritus Professor Rene Dubos. Both the introduction and the body of the book leave no doubt as to the power of the human mind in the healing process.

Apart from recognising the production of neuropeptides (which have already been considered in this chapter), Dubos identifies two more of the body's responses to this chemical production as influenced by the mind.

The first is the fighting of disease. The capacity of the body to produce antibodies and T cells in order to fight infection is influenced by the state of mind. He highlights the effect of hypnotic suggestion on the body's activity, as demonstrated when hypnosis was used with patients participating in the Mantoux test, stating that "Hypnotic suggestions can obliterate the vascular manifestations of the Mantoux test."[10] This test is used to determine the body's likely response to tuberculosis infection. Dubos finds this response to hypnosis to be "as neat a proof as one could wish of the influence that the mind exerts over the body."[10]

The second is the digestion of food. Dubos provides evidence that anxiety will slow down the biochemical process involving the breakdown of fat particles by appropriate enzymes. At a layman level, we commonly recognise that when someone is anxious, they will frequently choose different foods to when they are feeling relaxed. Perhaps this is our intuitive response to our body's digestive state at the time.

Dubos summarises by saying that the will to live mobilises the body's natural mechanisms of resistance to disease. He says that ancient physicians named this *vis medicatrix naturae*—the healing power of nature. Allowed to flourish, he believes that this natural response may be so effective that most challenges do not result in disease.

Cousins' detailed analysis and reflections deserve inclusion at this point as they provide a succinct exposé to many important considerations.

The Illness and His Cure

In 1964, Norman Cousins suffered from a degenerative disease involving the disintegration of the connective tissue of his spine, potentially caused by heavy metal poisoning and believed to be progressive and incurable. His own analysis led him to believe the disease was able to take hold of his body because he had adrenal gland exhaustion, making him vulnerable to the toxic shock from heavy metal exposure. This gland failure meant his endocrine system and hence his immune system were both not functioning well. He believed reversing this adrenal exhaustion was critical to his recovery.

Cousins then references Hans Selye's *The Stress of Life,* where he showed that adrenal exhaustion could be caused by emotional tension, such as frustration or rage, detailing the negative effects of negative emotions on body chemistry. With this realisation and armed with enormous self-will and the support of his doctor, Cousins set about changing his entire treatment program for the disintegration of the connective tissue of his spine. This included tangible, physical changes, such as ceasing his medication, leaving hospital and being cared for in a hotel room, and eating a nutritious diet. It also included an onslaught into his own thoughts and state of mind.

In order to stop taking painkillers, Cousins chose to work on his state of mind and embarked on a program calling for the full exercise of the affirmative emotions of hope, love, faith, and happiness as a factor in enhancing body chemistry. This began with watching amusing movies and having humour books read to him. This showed that ten minutes of genuine belly laughter had an anaesthetic effect and provided him with two hours of pain free sleep allowing the body to begin its healing process naturally with this rest. Cousins also believed that his partnership with his doctor, including the belief and commitment in the treatment program, was an important part of his on-going improvement.

As nutritional support, Cousins chose ascorbic acid (Vitamin C) in large doses to replace his other medications on the basis that it could help to oxygenate the blood, believing that impaired oxygenation was a factor in collagen breakdown, which was resulting in the disintegration of his connective tissue. Within eight days, his recovery became tangible with the ability to move his thumbs without pain. This statement in itself demonstrates the enormity of his body's degeneration and the low base from which he was working. At the point of writing fifteen years later, he was horse riding, playing the organ, playing tennis and golf, all without pain, although some body movements were still not fully recovered.

When recording his conclusions from the entire experience, Cousins believed that his personal experience and other research showed that the human being's will to live "is not a theoretical abstraction"[19] but rather that it had both physiologic with therapeutic characteristics. In support of this perspective, he also noted that his own strong, personal belief and the commitment of his doctor to that belief were of paramount importance to his own recovery.

The Power of the Placebo

Cousins discusses the influence of the placebo as a demonstration of the power of our thoughts in combating illness.

> *Cousins refers to the placebo as "the doctor who resides within."*[11]

He cites numerous doctors who have studied the effect of placebos as an authentic therapeutic agent for altering body chemistry. These examples range from reducing tremors in people suffering Parkinson's disease to providing relief from bleeding ulcers and arthritic pain, as well as overall health and longevity improvements. According to Cousins, some researchers believe that placebos activate the cerebral cortex in the brain, which in turn switches on the endocrine system in general and the adrenal glands in particular. Conversely, the cerebral cortex can also stimulate negative biochemical changes just as it does positive changes.

He describes the placebo as the initiator of a process beginning with the patient's confidence and extending through to the full functioning of his own immune and healing system. To Cousins, the human body is its own best apothecary, with the most successful prescriptions filled by the body itself.

In an article in *Scientific American*, Rachael Moeller describes the famous study conducted by Dr Bruce Moseley and his colleagues where 180 patients were randomly allocated to one of three different groups for their knee surgeries. All groups undertook exactly the same arthroscopic surgery. One group had the knee cartilage scraped away. One group had any loose knee cartilage flushed away. The third group did not have any action taken with the knee, other than to undertake the same surgical process to access the knee. "The results show that at every point in the investigation, all three groups reported an equal degree of reduction in pain and increase in activity level. Moseley and his collaborators thus conclude that the placebo effect can account for the observed improvements; the surgeries do not appear to have any significant effect on the actual physiology of the disease."[12]

For Cousins, "The placebo is proof that there is no separation between mind and body."[13] Illnesses can occur, first beginning in the mind and then affecting the body, or conversely first occurring in the body and ultimately affecting the mind. He supports this perspective by highlighting that both are served by the same bloodstream and stating that treating diseases as either physical or mental in isolation "must be considered archaic in the light of new evidence about the way the human body functions."[13]

Modern Search for the Tangible

As we search in our modern world for everything to be tangible before we accept it as being real, we deny ourselves the opportunity to consider that possibly, just possibly, there is something else in our being that brings all these biomechanical characteristics together to make humans what we are. To Cousins, letting go of the tangible is an essential element of our ability to self-heal.

> *"If we can liberate ourselves from tangibles, we can connect hope and the will to live directly to the ability of the body to meet great threats and challenges."*[14]

Perhaps that intangible commodity is the human spirit. Cousins refers to Dr Jerome D. Frank when he addressed medical graduates as far back as 1975. Dr Frank said, "Any treatment of an illness that does not administer to the human spirit is grossly deficient."[15]

How far have we moved from such forms of treatment today?

Cousins believes that this relationship between doctor and patient is the most powerful of healing agents, as it influences the patient's state of mind. He emphasises this point with a challenge to our modern technological approach to healing, quoting cardiologist Dr Bernard Lown: "An important principle in a person's ability to heal is 'the laying on of hands'—a practice that is rapidly atrophying because physicians are too busy with a 'laying on of tools.'"[16]

As a society, we have available to us a plethora of information from a range of different sources that point us towards the need for a rethink of the way we look at and attempt to manipulate the human body. We seem to have an obsession with the cleverness of technological intervention, such as pharmaceuticals and surgery as the major ways of healing the human body. I think that pharmaceuticals in particular may potentially be responsible for ailing the human body, not only through their direct ingestion but also from the impact of pharmaceuticals applied to the food we eat and to our farming land as discussed in earlier chapters. I think these technologies are frequently embraced as a quick fix, without due regard for the intricacies of the body's self-healing mechanisms.

It is these self-healing mechanisms that should be at the top of the list when it comes to the battery of options to heal an illness or condition.

Such options extend also to the influence on our genes from the food that we eat, as well as our thoughts and our environment. Not only does each person's food consumption, thoughts, and environment impact his or her own life but it appears they also impact the lives of their future descendants.

For me, the journey of discovery to this point has been most enlightening with respect to our food, our farming, the synergistic powers of nature, and the parallel lives of the health of the human body with the earth's soils. The linkages seem undeniable. Until now, it has been a journey of understanding of the whole and the impact of neglecting that whole from a cellular perspective.

> *As I have uncovered these snippets of information, joining the dots has been very confronting to me, to my life, and to the life of our family.*

As confronting as it has been, when I have taken the time to reflect and really absorb this information, these connections have also made sense and seemed relatively obvious to me.

My on-going journey has taken me to a new level of understanding and awe. I have come to appreciate that it is not only the physical aspects of our existence that impact on our well-being. Our thoughts, our food, our water, and the air we breathe are paramount to our health and to the health of the planet. Respect for these and the pursuit of these is vital. In addition, there is something more that is available to us that we can tap into to help the healing process for ourselves and for our landscape and to help to build our on-going well-being.

Part Two

Now this story moves beyond our farm. It moves beyond our realisations of the links between food and farming, between the health of our soil and the health of the human race and the impact of the environment on our DNA. These are big concepts to tackle in and of themselves.

> *I believe there is more. We physically exist in a world that is more than physical.*

Now it is time to return to the question: "If we are so dependent on the earth, are we really separate from it?"

I have already described that I think we are more than a bunch of cells working together in some mechanistic manner. We are that and more. Is it our spirit? Is it our consciousness? Whatever it is, we can't see it or measure it tangibly. But I am sure that it's there, and I am increasingly recognising the power of its influence. That influence was there on the farm. We didn't recognise it, so we couldn't really take advantage of it. For humans, I choose the word consciousness, as it seems to be widely accepted. What it really is and how it operates is a constant discussion. Nonetheless, it serves as a basis to help explore the power of the human mind and its influence on our health and well-being.

For all the thinking that we do as humans, I believe that we must be evolving in a positive way. I think we are also going full circle, as the saying goes. There is a shift in the way we interact with our earth and with each other. A glance at the healing power of the energies of our universe, including our own intuition, help to provide a springboard for the future. New possibilities really do exist to turn the tide on the health of our planet and ourselves.

> *Instead of "dominate or die," it could in fact be the opposite—if we dominate, we will die.*

For me, this is an enlightening journey of discovery, starting to piece together future possibilities and to experience for myself some of the wonders of the universe available to us all, beyond our physical presence on the planet.

Delving into the world of consciousness and the powers of the universe inevitably takes one closer to the questions asked by the spiritual leaders and interpretation of the spiritual messages that have abound in man's time on earth. As part of our going full circle, I think this also takes us back to the intersection between science and spirituality. It may be that some readers will interpret the following chapters not as stories about the power of the universe, its magnetic pull, and the influence of its vibrations but rather as stories about the power of prayer, our connection with a higher being, and the presence of the natural order of things. On this distinction, I pose no argument. For me, they are two sides of the same coin. Exploring these different interpretations in detail is for another time.

Although the following chapters are less tangible than the first section of the book, I have actually chosen the most tangible explanation I can harness in order to help to demonstrate the extraordinary powers of nature and their capacity to heal when allowed to do so. For some, these powers are spiritual. For others, they are powers of the universe. As humans, we have the ability to distinguish and analyse, thus developing our own perspective.

Chapter 6

Subtle Energy ... It's Not So Subtle

Energy exists in various forms. To continue to explore the sources of energy, we must return briefly to the logic and reasoning we are using in this debate about human health, soil health, and many other aspects of our modern lives. Controlled scientific experiments and controlled economic models allow us to identify cause and effect in a linear manner. Our propensity to often only accept as valid anything that can be proven in this way may be an indication that we have forgotten what we once knew instinctively and from observation about the influence of the whole.

Joseph Chilton Pearce likens our propensity to managing the parts rather than working from the whole as the separation of our intellect from our natural intelligence. "Intellect cut off from the intelligence of the whole becomes cancerous and begins to destroy the whole structure itself."[24] From Chilton Pearce's perspective, the intelligence roles of the brain and the heart are very distinct. He considers the heart as the source of our universal intelligence, and he considers the brain as the source of our individual intellect. The real success of the human, as Chilton Pearce sees it, is in the balance between the universal aspects of the heart and the individual aspects of our brain. This is not to dismiss the importance of the individual intellect but rather to utilise it in coherence with our universal intelligence. He holds strongly to the view that an important characteristic of our individual intellect is the ability to retrace thoughts and decisions to understand how we arrived at a particular situation. We are now at a point in time in the evolution of man and our place on this earth where that ability to retrace our thoughts and decisions is of paramount significance. How have we arrived at this state of imbalance?

Acknowledging the heart as the true seat of the mind is a rather bold concept from a modern perspective. Perhaps reawakening our awareness and access to the heart and its universal intelligence may be the avenue that allows us to continue to benefit from our huge advances in individual intellect and at the same time move towards a possibility of balance with our place on the earth.

> *It is worth considering whether our enthusiasm for the advancement of the individual intellect has allowed it to dominate our universal intelligence.*

Our focus on individual intellect has certainly driven the development of our sophisticated analysis tools and our capacity to break everything down into its component parts. These discoveries have provided the people of the world with a mass of information. For us to ultimately benefit from this information and continue to advance, the universal intelligence of the heart may need to surface again to re-establish coherence between man and the earth on which we depend.

We will return to the role of the heart later in this chapter. For now, a little more retrace-ability of our modern thinking could help to advance our understanding.

These sophisticated analysis tools combined with our increasing ability to break everything down into its component parts have led us to believing that we can manipulate these parts in isolation, forgetting that they are all interconnected with so much else.

A brief look at some of the work of two of the world's most famous physicists, Isaac Newton and Albert Einstein, can help to explain some of these differences in the development of our modern thinking and hence our frameworks for analysis and decision making.

By definition, a linear system must be additive. In this model, if any of the component parts are separated and manipulated, the result that is believed to be achieved by each part is then added to show the sum of the manipulation of all the component parts. Mathematically, this can be demonstrated by the following formula:

$$F(x) + F(y) + F(z) = F(x+y+z)$$

Reductionism, too, has some similar characteristics. Reductionism in science says that a complex system can be explained by reducing it to its fundamental parts.

Isaac Newton's classical mechanics and laws of motion revolutionised the study of physics. It would be folly to challenge the enormity of his contribution to modern science. However, the extent to which his principles of mechanics have been applied to modern medicine (and then to other organic systems) is one potential explanation for the medical tendency to consider the human body solely from a biomechanical perspective.

Modern medicine is often accused of offering pharmacological or surgical intervention to symptoms, basing its assumptions on this biomechanical perspective. It is not unreasonable to conclude, as many critics of modern medicine have done, that this method of medical practice is focusing on the parts rather than the whole in its diagnosis and treatment. So, too, could you conclude that similar reasoning with a predominantly linear, reductionist approach has been applied to the analysis and decision making of our food-production systems and the nurturing of our soils.

Albert Einstein had a different view. Regarded as the most influential physicist of the twentieth century, Einstein held the view that all matter is energy. His perspective developed into the relatively new field of physics known as quantum physics. It certainly turns on its head the biomechanical view of the natural world. (You may recall attempts were made by Albert Frank in 1885 to challenge this biomechanical view, with his discovery of the role of mycorrhizal fungi and its symbiotic relationship with the roots of plants.)

One of Einstein's famous quotes is appropriate to offer at this stage.

> *"Not everything that can be counted counts; and not everything that counts can be counted."*

A new swathe of philosophers, scientists, and medical practitioners is gradually emerging on the shirttails of Einstein's quantum world.

Neurosurgeon Eben Alexander, MD holds the view that the ascendance of the scientific method based solely in the physical realm over the past four hundred years presents a major problem: we have lost touch with the deep mystery at the centre of existence—our consciousness. Dr Alexander's view was formed after decades of operating on the human brain and understanding it at a physical and biomechanical level. He developed this expanded perspective following his own odyssey whilst in a seven-day coma, having suffered severe bacterial meningitis. There was no prospect that he would recover from this severe infection of the brain, but he returned to full health within three months and recorded his journey. Dr Alexander holds the view that our consciousness is at the centre of our existence, separate to our mechanical bodily functions, including the physical brain. His explanation is that our consciousness is our observer or awareness of our existence separate to our physical existence.

Richard Gerber is a western trained medical doctor whose focus for the past twenty years has shifted to research and writing in the field of vibrational medicine. Gerber is emphatic that the majority of biological researchers and physicians are still working from a Newtonian model of living systems in which the human body is seen as a cellular mechanism. Gerber is critical of conventional medical approaches. He says that these conventional approaches are based on the notion that physical repair and the elimination of abnormal cellular systems can cure all illnesses. Gerber holds the Einsteinium view that matter is energy and that humans are beings of energy. To Gerber, "The body would be but a pile of disordered chemicals were it not for the animating life-force that maintains and organises our molecular substituents into living, breathing, thinking individuals."[25] Gerber believes that this life force is present in and animates from all living creatures.

If we accept this modern interpretation and experimentation of Einstein's principles as valid, then we must come to the view that there is something more to the life of the elements of nature than their physical molecular structure. That quest for a particular type of evidence may be what's holding back our progress in this field. Gerber explains that physicians do not deal with these subtle forces, which he believes are so evident and so influential in our lives and well-being, because current scientific models cannot explain their existence of function.

Biologist Rupert Sheldrake is very positive about man's growing awareness. His view is that: "It's already happening. It's a move towards a more organic view of nature, a more interconnected view of nature—where we see nature, the whole universe, the earth and living organisms, not as machines."[26]

Subtle energy is one such nonphysical phenomenon. Returning to Gerber's reference to spirit, one anonymous description of it helps to pave the way for our discussion about subtle energy.

"Spirit … you can't touch it, but you can feel it; you can't stop it, but you can start it; you can't contain it, but you can carry it with you wherever you go."

The Vibrations of Colour, Sound, and Thought

Dr Patrick MacManaway is a Scottish-born, western-trained medical practitioner and also a second-generation esoteric healer. Dr MacManaway has developed both a rational and metaphysical understanding of these two diverse perspectives—the biomechanical world and the quantum world. In addition to his western medical training, he has built a deep historic knowledge of ancient energetic practices and is able to map the languages to modern scientific terminology. His explanation makes the concept of energy almost tangible, if not tangible in itself.

To explain the existence of subtle energy—that is, energy that exists but cannot be seen—Dr MacManaway begins by focusing on our knowledge of the presence of electromagnetism in and around the earth. His first point of reference is the two different electrical currents we are familiar with—direct charge (DC) and alternating charge (AC) currents.

A direct current is seen by us when we consider a simple bar magnet. Using a compass, we identify a magnet as having a north pole and a south pole. Still with the compass, we can also plot the pathway of the energy from the northern point to the southern point of the magnet. This is a curved, flowing pattern of multiple paths of energy. This energy cannot really be *seen*. To the human eye, it is invisible. Yet we know it exists because we can see the *effect* of the energy and the presence of the pathways, demonstrated most graphically with the use of iron filings. The path formed by the iron filings clearly demonstrates the flow of energy between the opposing polarities of the magnets.

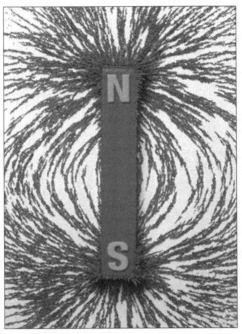

Illustration 5. Demonstration of magnetism using
iron filings with a standard bar magnet.

The current is constant and always flows in the same direction from positive to negative, from north to south—hence the term "direct current." We also use this current when we manufacture batteries, with the two polarities identified by the + and − symbols printed at opposite ends of the battery. For example, to provide energy to the light of a torch, the positive terminal connects to a piece of metal, allowing the two polarities to form a conductive loop, supplying energy to the torch.

In the same way as the magnet demonstrates, when we use a compass as a geographic navigational tool on the earth's surface, we focus our efforts on identifying north (N) on the compass. This N is pointing us to the magnetic force of the North Pole, the positive charge. Right across the earth, you can determine the north and south polarities using a compass. The energy flowing between the North and South Poles can be represented in the same way as the energy flowing between the two poles of a bar magnet, once again a DC current.

The other current that occurs naturally on the earth's surface is an alternating current (AC). Nicola Tesla discovered the existence of this alternating current in the late 1800s. This current dances back and forth between positive and negative charges to form a wave. The current is formed by the influence of the sun's solar wind in the resonate space around the earth. The solar wind emits charged particles that are pushing against the earth's magnetic field. This creates a micro-pulsation in the cavity between the earth and the layer of atmosphere called the ionosphere. The earth is negatively charged, and the ionosphere is positively charged. The micro-pulsation creates a range of different waves known as the Schumann Resonances, which can be thought of as the solar wind beating its pulse on earth. The lowest frequency of these waves is 7.83 Hz. This frequency is of particular importance when we look further at the notion of our connectedness to the earth.

The movement created by these waves, or AC currents, flows around the cavity between the earth and the ionosphere. This alternating current connects with the energy from the direct current (DC) that is flowing between the earth's two magnetic poles. When these two different types of currents combine at a particular electrical level, their charge in the atmosphere creates lightning strikes.

Earlier in the book, we looked at the natural occurrence of nitrogen in the atmosphere through lightning strikes. When it comes to our natural food system, this nitrogen is fixed from the atmosphere by legume plants, which grow nodules on their roots in order to capture the nitrogen and make it available to the soil. Both are quite limited in nature's cycle. It was man's manufacture of artificial nitrogen that formed a foundation for large increases in the production of food, allowing for our population explosion as witnessed for the past sixty years.

The concept of electricity is also familiar to us, most commonly recognised as a source of power harnessed through industrial processes from renewable and non-renewable resources, such as the sun, water, wind, coal, and natural gas. Electricity also occurs naturally through the combination of both AC and DC currents in the atmosphere. We can't see the electricity, but we can harness its power and feel its effects.

Just as there is invisible energy flowing through and around the earth, so too there is energy flowing through and around the human body. Dr MacManaway explains that the heart is the primary source of electromagnetic energy in humans. The mitochondria in each cell create the electromagnetic charge, which then provides the energy for the heart to beat. Much as the DC and AC currents combine to form the energy on the earth, so too do they combine to form the energy of the human body. The magnetic field created by the heart is an identical but smaller version of the magnetic field around the earth.

The brain is thought to amplify and resonate to the frequencies generated from the heart and from external sources such as the earth's beat.

This electromagnetism is not static. It has currents that change constantly depending on our position in relation to the sun and other planets. The earth's very dynamic field is constantly changing around us and is mirrored in a dynamic way by the field we carry inside us. Dieter Broers provides a highly comprehendible explanation of this phenomenon in his documentary titled *Solar Revolution*, where he highlights the impact of the solar system on the organisms on earth, emphasising its influence on humans at many levels of consciousness.

Electromagnetism is a medium like air or water, which all hold and conduct vibrations. To measure this vibration, modern physics uses wavelength and frequency. The wavelength is the length of the wave of a vibration, typically measured from the point between the two peaks of the wave. It is measured in metres. The frequency is the number of times the wave occurs within a given time frame. This is generally measured as waves or cycles per second, known as Hertz (Hz). As the frequency intensifies, the wavelength becomes shorter, allowing more waves to occur in the given time.

Sound waves occur in a range of frequencies, as do light waves. We only hear some of the sound waves, and we only see some of the light waves. Although many of these light and sound waves are not actually detectable by humans, we know they exist because of the sophistication of the measurement techniques that have been developed and because we can often see the effects rather than the field itself.

Humans can hear sound waves roughly in the range between 100 Hz and 20,000 Hz. Dogs, by contrast, typically respond to sound frequencies as high as 40,000 to 50,000 Hz.

The range of colour that we perceive is also only a small portion of the frequencies that are emitted by the earth's electromagnetic energy. The human colour spectrum is represented by the colours of the rainbow, which range in frequency from approximately 380 to 770 THz (1 THz is equivalent to 10^{12} or 1 trillion Hz). The wavelength range of this same colour spectrum is from 780 to 390 nanometres. (One nanometre is equivalent to one billionth of a metre). This means that of the colours that we can detect, violet has the shortest wavelength with the highest frequency, and red has the longest wavelength with the lowest frequency. There are waves that exist beyond our visible colour spectrum. Just beyond violet, outside our visible spectrum, are the ultraviolet rays. At the other end of our visible spectrum are the infrared rays, which exist as waves beyond the colour red. We cannot see either of these, but we can feel their effects; UV rays burn us, and infrared rays are used by modern technology to observe the presence of humans and animals in the dark without the subject sensing or seeing the light.

Putting these sounds and colours in the context of being outside our capacity to detect them helps to demonstrate the notion that a wide range of vibrations influence us, but we are not necessarily aware of them directly. The range of waves that has been measured can be seen on this diagram produced by NASA, ranging from radio waves, which measure longer than one metre, to gamma rays, which measure smaller than a nanometre. This diagram highlights the relatively small spectrum of visible light to the human eye.

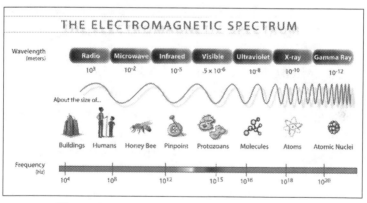

Illustration 6. The electromagnetic spectrum.[9]

Another way to understand the influence of these unseen waves is to consider X-rays and their use for medical imagery. It is widely acknowledged that X-rays can have a deleterious impact on the human body, hence the use of appropriate screening for the operators who are constantly exposed to the rays, and also the caution advised for pregnant women, for children, and for excessive use on one person. The X-ray, when projected, travels through the body to allow the image of the target area to be created. This is one example of an electromagnetic wave that we know travels through the body and impacts its function. If we accept this as being true, and we accept that all electromagnetic waves are on a spectrum as illustrated, it seems reasonable to also accept that all electromagnetic waves, or vibrations, could influence the human body.

> *To recap, colour and sounds are both vibrations. It is the wavelength and frequency of these vibrations that determines whether we define them as colours or sounds. Regardless of which they are, they still influence aspects of our bodily function and hence our actual well-being.*

By way of simple example, modern light bulbs and blue-screened mobile devices emit a frequency of light that slows down the release of the hormone melatonin in our brains. This affects our sleep patterns and our moods by interrupting our circadian body rhythms and hence our state of health.

Colours and sounds are just the beginning of the power of vibrations. A change in the understanding and use of these powerful tools is possible. There is a vast amount of knowledge available to build a modern understanding within our communities of the ability of the body to self-manage and self-heal.

It is a very exciting and empowering prospect.

The heart, the brain and the power of it all

Returning now to the heart.

Expressions that are familiar to us such as "she died of a broken heart" and "he had a heart attack because of the stress he was under" are recognised at a layman's level in our society as feasible cause-and-effect scenarios. However, when it comes to treating illnesses, our medical system most frequently seems to revert to the pharmacological model of treatment.

Modern evidence supporting a change in approach seems to be surfacing.

The Institute of HeartMath cites landmark long-term studies conducted at the University of London by Dr Hans Eysenck showing that chronic unmanaged emotional stress is as much as six times more predictive of cancer and heart disease than cigarette smoking, cholesterol level, or blood pressure and much more responsive to intervention.

One measure of stress identified by the Institute of HeartMath is a person's heart rate variability (HRV). Managing this HRV may be an underutilised key to human health at many levels. HRV is the difference in the rhythm that occurs between individual heartbeats. While your heart may be beating at a healthy rate of perhaps seventy beats per minute, there may be a high variability of rhythm *between* each of those beats. The normal range in heartbeat is due to the synergistic action of the two branches of the autonomic nervous system. This represents the net effect of the sympathetic and parasympathetic nervous systems of speeding up and slowing down the heart rate depending on the stimulus. Mental and emotional stress increases sympathetic activity, commonly known as the fight/flight response. By contrast, feelings of calmness and clarity generate parasympathetic activity, slowing down the heartbeat and allowing the body to regenerate. Sleep also provides ideal conditions for the parasympathetic nervous system to operate. Further than the measure of the heart beat itself, achieving a coherent rhythm between each heart beat (heart rate variability) appears to be a critical factor in allowing the body's major systems to synchronize their activities.

The Institute of HeartMath has defined physiological coherence as a state characterised by four major features: high heart rhythm coherence (sine wavelike rhythmic pattern); increased parasympathetic activity; increased entrainment and synchronization between physiological systems; and efficient and harmonious functioning of the cardiovascular, nervous, hormonal, and immune systems. They have found that in states in which there is a high degree of coherence within the HRV waveform, there also tends to be increased coherence between the rhythmic patterns produced by different physiological oscillatory systems (e.g., synchronization and entrainment between heart rhythms, respiratory rhythms, and blood pressure oscillations).

Respiratory rhythms are of particular interest here, as they can be consciously controlled. That control can have significant impact on the other bodily systems. In the first instance, they modulate the pattern of the heart rhythms. When we breathe at a slow, rhythmic rate, we can facilitate coherence and entrainment. The reverse appears to also be true. We are normally not conscious of our breathing. It seems that our breath is often influenced by and synchronized to the cardiac cycle. Changes in emotional states also alter breathing rates. When we are agitated, our breathing becomes faster and shallower. When we experience positive emotional states, our breathing slows down, and we breathe deeper. According to the Institute of HeartMath, "These emotion-related changes in breathing are likely to result, at least in part, from changes in input from the cardiovascular centers."[27]

Combining an awareness of calm, conscious breathing while you visualise the breath going in and out through your heart, at the same time as focusing attention on generating a positive emotion for yourself, can develop a smooth, coherent heart rhythm for an extended period of time. As previously discussed, this coherence strengthens the physiological patterns of coherence and synchronization within the body. Calm, conscious breath and positive thoughts are the two ingredients that are available to us to easily drive healthy changes to our own bodies.

Without heart rhythm coherence, synchronization of the body's major systems is diminished. The emotional state of the person can determine the degree of heart rhythm coherence, as demonstrated in these two diagrams.

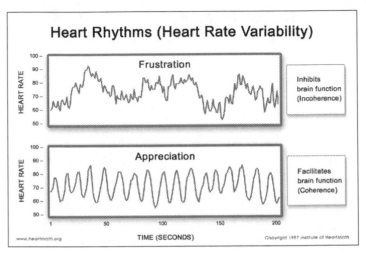

Illustration 7. Changes in heart rhythm coherence in the different emotional states of appreciation and frustration.[10]

When the person is experiencing frustration, the HRV is random and erratic. This contrasts with the clear pattern of coherence achieved through feelings of love and appreciation.

Two aspects of our natural healing powers are highlighted in these HRV observations. Firstly, if it is that heart rhythm coherence is so influential on the rhythmic function of our body's internal systems, what could be its level of influence on our overall well-being? Secondly, if it is that our thoughts influence our bodily function, then what is the influence of our thoughts and feelings on this same well-being? These experiments appear to show that our thoughts and feelings affect our HRV, which then affects our body's autonomic nervous system and oscillatory systems, which logically affect our overall well-being.

So what is it about our thoughts and feelings that generate such a dramatic influence on our heart? We have previously discussed the vibrations of colour and sound and their potential influence. Similarly, thoughts and feelings also emit a vibration, and it is this vibration that appears to influence the heart and the brain in a range of interconnected bodily functions.

An internationally renowned musician and neuroscientist has advanced man's understanding of the shape of emotions by combining his two fields of knowledge. Born in Austria and brought up in Australia, Dr Clynes spent many years conducting his research at Rockdale Mental Hospital in New York in the 1960s. It was here that he invented a device that records the individual shape of different emotions. Dr Clynes named these shapes "essentic forms" of emotion. The basic human emotions he has recorded include (among others) anger, hate, love, and joy. Dr Clynes's device measures finger pressure for two seconds while the subject is fantasising the experience of the particular emotion. This fantasising is achieved by imagining a situation where the person would experience this emotion. The resultant graphs show a distinct difference in finger pressure depending on the emotion being experienced, and hence a distinct difference in the shape of this emotion. His experiments showed a consistent shape to each emotion across different cultural groups, testing people from Bali, Indonesia, Mexico, Japan, and the United States. The only differences were when the words for an emotion did not have an exact translation.

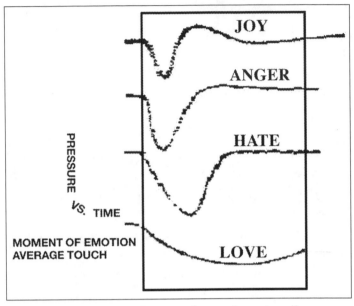

Illustration 8. The waveforms of emotions.[11]

Much like the research findings from the Institute of HeartMath, the participants in Dr Clynes's research found that regular practice of fantasising the range of different emotions resulted in improved well-being. This includes a greater inner peace for up to twenty-four hours, a heightened sense of calm, an improved sense of belonging, and a sense of being glad to be alive. Dr Clynes also reported that this experience can help to relieve pain, insomnia, and mild forms of depression.

Dr Clynes also believes that the shape of our emotions are so much a part of us that famous artists such as Picasso use these shapes intuitively while creating a piece of art, assisting them to evoke emotion in their work. As a concert pianist himself, he noticed that different pieces evoked different emotional responses from his audiences. He also discovered that certain emotional shapes consistently arose when people listened to great classical music.

To Dr Clynes, the shape of the emotion is as much a part of your body as the shape of your nose. We can see and measure the dimensions of the shape of the nose, and with this technology, we can also see and measure the dimensions of the shape of each emotion. The emotion, however, only appears at points in time, whereas the nose has a constant physical presence. To Dr Clynes, this presence only existent in time does not diminish the importance of our emotions and their capacity to influence the body. Dr Clynes's view is that music moves us not only emotionally but bodily as well.

It seems that the heart influences not only the function of our major bodily systems but also the brain, potentially to a greater level than the brain influences the heart.

The concept of the "heart brain" was introduced to modern science in 1991 by Dr J. Andrew Armour. He concluded that the heart has a complex intrinsic nervous system that is sufficiently sophisticated to qualify as a "little brain" in its own right. This heart brain has an elaborate circuitry, which enables it to act independently of the cranial brain—to learn, remember, and even feel and sense. Hormonal, chemical, rate, and pressure information is translated into neurological impulses by the heart's nervous system and sent from the heart to the brain. According to the Institute of HeartMath, the heart has its own intrinsic nervous system that operates and processes information independently of the brain or the body's commonly recognised nervous system.

Cyndi Dale writes: "Most people believe that the brain initiates the first response to incoming events and then orders our reactions. Analysis reveals, however, that incoming information first impacts the heart, and through the heart, the brain and then the rest of the body."[28]

The heart is the most powerful generator of electromagnetic energy and rhythmic information patterns in the human body. With every beat, the heart not only pumps blood but also transmits complex patterns of neurological, hormonal, pressure, and electromagnetic information to the brain and throughout the body. "The heart's electrical field is about 60 times greater in amplitude than the electrical activity generated by the brain. This field, measured in the form of an electrocardiogram (ECG), can be detected anywhere on the surface of the body. Furthermore, the magnetic field produced by the heart is more than 5,000 times greater in strength than the field generated by the brain, and can be detected a number of feet away from the body, in all directions, using SQUID-based magnetometers." [29]

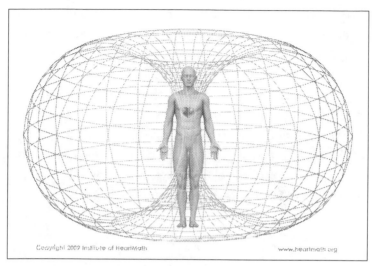

Copyright 2007 Institute of HeartMath   www.heartmath.org

Illustration 10. The electromagnetic field of the heart.[12]

The Institute of HeartMath concludes from its extensive research that the heart communicates information as reflected by the patterns of the body's heart rate variability. This information is communicated to the cardiac centre of the brain stem, which then feeds this information to parts of the brain connected to the base of the frontal lobes, areas considered critical to decision making and the integration of reason and feeling. To the Institute of HeartMath, this research provides "a pathway and mechanism to explain how the heart's rhythms can alter brainwave patterns and thereby modify brain function."[30]

Just as an electrocardiogram (ECG) is used to measure heart beat and heart rate variability, an electroencephalogram (EEG) records the tiny electrical impulses produced by the brain's activity. The most frequently measured impulses range from less than 3.75 Hz (cycles per second) to 30 Hz. The brain works in different frequencies during different phases of consciousness. As explained by Dr MacManaway, each shift in sleep state is also an octave of frequency, with a geometric model of doubling appearing inside each range of brain waves. The level of consciousness gradually increases as the frequency of the brain wave activity increases, moving from deep, dreamless sleep to the acute awareness of our five senses in our physical, action-related world.

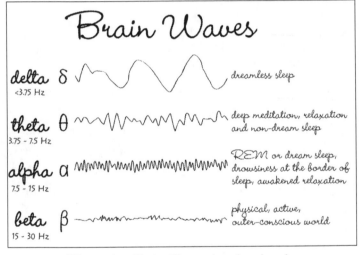

Illustration 11. An illustration showing the changes in the frequency and form of brain waves in differing states of consciousness.

The geometric midpoint of these four octaves is also the primary Schumann Resonance of 7.83 Hz. This frequency occurs within the alpha brainwaves, which range from 7.5 to 15 Hz. It is when we are in an alpha state that we are the most receptive to the rhythms of the heart. Not only are we receptive to the rhythms of our own heart, we are also receptive to the rhythms of other people's hearts. And so, we are indeed connected! We detect each other's heart rhythms through each other's brainwaves. These alpha brainwaves are most active when the person is in a state of awakened relaxation. Achieving this state of awakened relaxation can be aided by focused attention on your breathing patterns while shifting your conscious thoughts to a sincerely loving or caring state, generating a coherence in the waveform that represents the heart rate variance (HRV). Once again, like the roots of the plant and the mycorrhizal fungi, we are looking at a two-way trade.

For your brainwaves to be most receptive to the heart rhythm of another person, your own heart rhythms need to be in a state of internal coherence, assisted by conscious thoughts of sincere love.

It seems that the HRV response generated from focused breathing helps the establishment of loving and caring thoughts, which then develop a synchronicity between the brain and the heart, emitting vibrations that then influence the frequencies of the brain and the heart of others around them.

Data from the Institute of HeartMath showed that in subjects separated by several feet, synchronization can occur between the alpha waves in one person's brain rhythms, as measured by an EEG, and the other's heart rhythms, as measured by an ECG signal. The degree and effectiveness of this synchronization appears to be influenced by the degree of coherence in the receiving subject's heart rhythms. Subjects who demonstrated high heart rhythm coherence were more likely to show alpha wave synchronization to the other subject's ECG. This effect was not apparent in subjects with low heart rhythm coherence.

> *In summary, when people touch or are in proximity to each other, one person's heartbeat signal is registered in the other person's brainwaves.*

This interconnectedness of human beings with each other is widely accepted in many cultures and belief systems and is increasingly gaining acceptance at the edge of modern scientific thinking. Add to that the notion of our connectedness to other species and to the planet as a whole. In addition to these heart-based experiments, others have shown more graphically how our thoughts and beliefs transcend the limits of time and space as we know them.

Dr Cleve Backster was one such person. He was a polygrapher with the United States Central Intelligence Agency (CIA). After first identifying that plants respond to human emotions, he conducted a series of experiments demonstrating that human DNA responds to the emotion felt by the person, whether or not it is connected to the person's body. In Cleve Backster's experiments, white blood cells were separated out and placed in a separate vile. The subjects from whom the DNA had been removed then projected different spontaneous emotions based on looking at pictures, watching movies, communicating with family members by telephone, etc. Cleve Baxter conducted these experiments when the vile of DNA was located in several different locations, including in the same room, in another room in the same building as its host, within twenty-five kilometres, and when the host and the vial were separated by more than three hundred kilometres. There was no measureable difference in the extent of the response and no delay in the timing of the response. Regardless of distance, the response seemed instantaneous.

Despite the natural scepticism surrounding these experiments, even prior to some of his most profound findings, Dr Howard Miller, a cytologist (the branch of biology that deals with the formation, structure, and function of cells) stated that these findings may mean the discovery of "a kind of cellular consciousness."[31]

It seems that there is something within us, linked to the emotions and thoughts that we experience, that transcends the limits of time and space the way we understand them today.

This concept has been further demonstrated by some extraordinary experiments conducted by the Institute of HeartMath. Following on from the findings of Dr Cleve Backster, the Institute of HeartMath replicated some aspects of his work and included further additional considerations as well. These new experiments introduced the variable of intention into the focused thought. Applying their models of heart-coherence, the subjects were asked to move their minds and bodies to a coherent state and to include in their thoughts the intention of altering the structure of the DNA that had been placed in the separated vials.

The results give one cause to sit quietly and ponder the extraordinary.

Whether the vials of separated DNA were in the same room or whether they were one kilometre away, the subjects who combined the coherent state with the intention of altering the structure of the DNA were successful at doing so.

> *The conclusion from this result is that focused thoughts generated in a physiologically coherent state can alter the structure of DNA both inside and outside our body.*

This extraordinary information about vibrations and the power of our thoughts has drawn me to a most powerful point of realisation in my life.

> *I realise that at three levels I am a person of profound influence.*

Firstly, I directly influence my own physical and emotional well-being through my own thoughts and by making a choice about the people with whom I surround myself, being influenced also by their thoughts and attitudes. (We know that instinctively. This is simply explaining it from a different perspective.) Secondly, I can influence the lives of people around me through the vibrations that emanate from my being. Thirdly, and most profoundly, my own well-being influences the health and well-being of future offspring and subsequent generations. This is not only true for my offspring and their children but for everyone's offspring with whom I interact!

Everything about me influences everyone around me,
and then everyone around them, and on it goes.

For me, this is both daunting and inspiring in equal measure. I am a flawed human being, filled with feelings of uncertainty, intolerances, and imperfections. For all of this, my power is absolute. Making a choice to improve my life through my own actions and attitudes is the most powerful thing I can do for myself and for those who are dear to me. This choice that I make has an eternal ripple effect.

There are some very graphic examples available to us that show how our thoughts transcend the limits of time and space as we know it, existing and influencing everything everywhere. One such example is the work conducted by Dr Masaru Emoto where he demonstrates the influence of thought by showing its effects on the crystals in water. Amongst other works, Dr Emoto has published the most astounding photographs in his series of books titled *Messages in Water*. Dr Emoto discovered that the shape and clarity of crystals displayed in frozen water will be different, based on the concentrated thoughts directed towards them. He found that water exposed to loving words shows brilliant and complex patterns. By contrast, water that is exposed to negative and hateful thoughts develops crystals of completely different random designs, lacking form and complex qualities.

Dr Emoto used a range of different techniques to expose water to different thought patterns. Sometimes he wrapped a piece of paper with words typed on it around a bottle of water. Sometimes he conducted group sessions where a whole group of people would combine with focused thought at the same time, either thinking positive thoughts or thinking negative thoughts. On other occasions, those conducting the experiments would daily speak the words of the emotion to the water as they walked passed and watch the results over time. No matter which technique Dr Emoto chose, the same results occurred. Water responded to the thoughts, words, and emotions of those around it. That is, water responded to the vibrations.

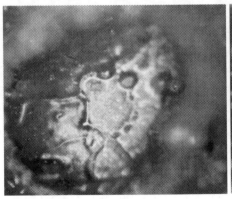 

Illustration 12a. Before
Buddhist prayer at
Fujiwara Dam, Japan

Illustration 12b. After
Buddhist prayer at
Fujiwara Dam, Japan

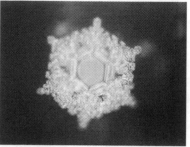

Illustration 12c. You make
me sick. I will kill you

Illustration 12d. Love
and gratitude

Illustration 12 (a-d). Water crystals exposed to
different emotions.[13]

These images demonstrate graphically the effect of
thought on water crystals. Images 12a and 12b show the
transformation of water crystals before and after focused
thought. In this example, the water is from a dam in Japan.
Image 12a is the water prior to any focused thoughts.
This contrasts dramatically with image 12b that shows
a pure crystal form developing after the Buddhist prayer.
The water crystals in images 12c and 12d have both
been exposed to focused thought. Image 12c has been
photographed after a focus of negative, hateful thoughts.
Image 12d forms an image of pure beauty after focused
thoughts of love and gratitude.

Dr MacManaway describes it this way. "Thought has
form and frequency. Emotion has form and frequency.
Water is a matrix that demonstrates that frequency."

What does this tell us about the power of our
vibrations? There are no limits to the answers to this

question. First and most obvious, our bodies are made up of more than 70 per cent water. It does not take a huge leap in logic to consider therefore the impact of our words, thoughts, and emotions on our own lives and the lives of those around us.

Dr MacManaway believes that the power of leverage of subtle energy through the human mind is almost boundless. Gregg Bradden is another enthusiastic and long-standing proponent of the power of subtle energy on our lives. He has authored a multitude of books and spoken internationally on different aspects of subtle energy for over a decade. His analysis of people's often-sceptical response to the use of subtle energy as a healing tool is an enlightening one. Gregg Bradden argues that it could be seen as a miracle if you did not accept the physics behind the occurrence. Once the physics is accepted, then such acts will be considered "available technology."[32]

We are each witness to our own well-being through our own thoughts and the thoughts of those with whom we interact.

This takes us back to the starting point of the electromagnetic fields that emanate from each of us. Dr MacManaway simplifies it this way. He says, "There is no difference between sunlight, your mobile phone signal and your thoughts. It is just a slower or faster beat."

Cyndi Dale authored a text titled *The Subtle Body*. In this book, she provides extraordinary detail regarding the energetic makeup of humans. In the introduction, she states, "Each cell pulses electrically, and the body itself emanates electromagnetic fields. The human body is a complex energetic system, composed of hundreds of energetic subsystems. Disease is caused by energetic imbalances." [33]

"We can't see all the energies that keep the body healthy, however. Those we can see are called physical, or measureable, energies. Those that we can't yet perceive are called subtle energies. Subtle doesn't mean delicate. In fact, science is beginning to suggest that the subtle … actually directs the measurable and forms our physical framework." [33]

And so continues our exploration of the presence of energy inside and outside our bodies.

The heart appears to be at the centre of many of the subtle energetic forces that influence our bodies. Dr MacManaway views the heart as the primary source of electromagnetic energy in humans. The brain is thought to amplify and resonate to the frequencies generated from the heart and from external sources, such as the earth's beat.

The earth's beat, as previously discussed, has its lowest vibration or resonance at 7.83 Hz. It seems to be no coincidence that this Schumann resonance of 7.83 Hz is the also at the lowest end of the resonance of our brain waves when we are operating in an alpha state—the state in which we are most receptive to the pulse of others.

How is all this relevant to our shift in consciousness regarding how we interact with the earth and with each other?

For me, coming to realise our interconnectedness at such a fundamental level gives me an explanation as to why nature's cycles are so important to our health. Discovering more ways to interact with these cycles seems paramount to our future place on earth. This goes for the choices we make with our foods, the choices we make with our thoughts, and the choices we make regarding our health regimes.

Subtle energy is around us. We cannot switch it off. We can learn to feel it, observe its effects, and tap into its benefits.

I will return to our family farm for a moment. The expressions "connected with the land" and "an eye for cattle" were often used by people to describe the skills of the grandmother of the family on our farm. We all understood and accepted what that meant. I recognise now that this skill was real and relates back to subtle energy—that these were forms of energetic awareness existent in our family as a natural part of our lives. In our case, our highly trained analytical minds overrode this intuition, and we made choices that we later recognised were not sustainable for the land or for us. Reigniting that intuition and acknowledging its application in many aspects of our modern lives allows us as people to combine our individual intellect (our brain) with our universal intelligence (our heart).

Chapter 7

A Place for Vibrational Medicine

If all these vibrations exist inside and outside our bodies, then what is their role in our lives, and what is their role in our bodies?

It seems that we are reacquainting ourselves with these ancient practices and redefining them as modern discoveries of vibrations and frequencies. One discipline of medicine that is emerging in our western societies is the discipline of vibrational medicine. It takes many different forms, all of which acknowledge the power of vibrations as healing frequencies when applied with focus and positive intent. This focus is possible as we return to our universal intelligence through our heart. The explanation for this discipline, though, is very brain based.

Richard Gerber's text, *Vibrational Medicine*, has now been published in more than eight languages, across eastern and western cultures. Gerber provides remarkable detail about his own journey into the world of vibrations, as well as modern scientific explanations behind many of these ancient concepts.

Gerber highlights the work of two scientists in the 1940s from different nations using different technologies and drawing similar conclusions. This work also takes us right back to the positive and negative polarities of the earth and shows how all living creatures mirror this electromagnetism. Harold S. Burr was researching at Yale University in the United States at the same time as the Russian researcher Semyon Kirlian was working halfway across the world. According to Gerber, both researchers discovered that diseases like cancer cause significant changes in the electromagnetic fields of living organisms. Burr measured micro-voltage levels to conduct his assessments. Kirlian developed imagery techniques originally known as electrography (and now known as Kirlian photography), showing electrical fields of living organisms accessing the holographic principles of nature, where one part of the body can be photographed, mirroring the electrical system of the entire body. (This notion of holographic principles in nature is used today in a very different application with cloning technologies taking a single unfertilised egg containing all the necessary DNA data for the entire creature to grow.)

Burr's work on the electromagnetism of living organisms led him to discover that the electrical axis aligned with the nervous system of the adult salamander was synonymous with the axis present in the unfertilised egg. This electrical axis is the same as that described earlier with a magnet and with the earth itself, with positive and negative magnetism at opposite ends of the axis. In addition, Burr discovered that the electrical field around a sprouted seed did not resemble the shape of the original seed but rather the shape of the fully grown plant. This research led him to the conclusion that "any developing organism was destined to follow a prescribed growth template and that such a template was generated by the organism's individual electromagnetic field."[34]

This is where the possibilities of vibrational healing start to appear a little more complicated. For some, this may be a bridge too far with respect to understanding and acceptance. Gerber provides a succinct summary of each chapter in his text. Some of the points he includes in his summary are listed here:[35]

- Most orthodox approaches to healing, including drugs and surgery, are based upon the Newtonian viewpoint that the human body is a complex machine.

- The Einsteinium viewpoint of vibrational medicine sees the human being as a multidimensional organism made up of physical/cellular systems in dynamic interplay with complex regulatory energetic fields. Vibrational medicine attempts to heal illness by manipulating these subtle-energy fields via directing energy into the body instead of manipulating the cells and organs through drugs or surgery.

- The etheric body is a holographic energy field or template that carries information for the growth, development, and repair of the physical body. While the genes within the DNA direct the molecular mechanisms that govern the development of individual cells, the etheric body guides the spatial unfoldment of the genetic process.

- The movement of the life force into the physiological/cellular systems is guided by the subtle patterns within the etheric body as well as by higher inputs into the human energetic system. Various vibrational healing modalities ... can influence these subtle patterns to improve human functioning and heal illness.

As research has progressed beyond Burr's original work, it is now claimed through a range of different sources that the existence of this subtle energy, having first appeared in the unfertilised egg, continues to exist throughout life, whether or not the physical element continues to exist, such as when someone has suffered a limb amputation. To explain this, Gerber refers to the discovery of a holographic energy template, known as the Phantom Leaf Phenomenon, which shows the continued presence of the etheric energy of the leaf even once part of the physical leaf has been broken off.

Layers of energy are present in our bodies simultaneous with our physical existence. To Richard Gerber and to Patrick MacManaway, it is only a difference in frequency that determines the difference between etheric matter and physical matter. They can exist in the same space, just as radio and television waves exist in the same space. They are only converted into waves we can see and hear by our own devices, such as radios and televisions.

In living organisms, these frequencies are more than just present. Many exist as layers of energy that give our physical body its form and function. According to Richard Gerber, the cellular growth of our physical matter is determined by the information carried on the etheric energetic map. It carries the spatial information on how the developing foetus is to unfold in utero and also the structural data for growth and repair of the adult organism should damage or disease occur. As Burr determined, the template of the salamander limb already exists and allows a new foot to grow if the present one is severed. "The physical body is so energetically connected and dependent upon the etheric body for cellular guidance that the physical body cannot exist without the etheric body. If the etheric field becomes distorted, physical disease soon follows. Many illnesses begin first in the etheric body and are then later manifested in the physical body as organ pathology."[36]

Gerber goes on to explain that the etheric body is not completely separated from the physical system with which it interacts. His view is that energetic information is able to flow from one system to another through specific channels that allow this energy exchange to occur.

Research into these concepts has been conducted using modern western measurement systems. This research supports the acknowledged ancient eastern literature of the existence of such systems. One of the better known is the meridian system, which is widely recognised as being part of Chinese medicine and also the central focus of acupuncture treatments. Gerber references research conducted by Korean professor Kim Bong Han in the 1960s, identifying that the meridian system not only interlinks within itself but appears to interconnect with all cell nuclei of the tissues. In addition, Kim determined that the meridian ducts of an embryonic chic are formed within fifteen hours of conception.

Combining the findings of these three researchers over more than two decades from Russia, the United States, and Korea, Gerber concludes that the spatial organisation of growth, from the formation and development of the embryo through to its maturity in adulthood, is guided by a template of a holographic energy field, known as the etheric body. This etheric body exists within a range of frequencies that coexist with the frequencies that make up the physical body and influence the growth and health of that physical body.

Gerber continues throughout his text to espouse that there are indeed many types of subtle energy bodies connected with the physical form. From Gerber's interpretation, each type has its own range of frequencies, much like octaves of a piano keyboard, with the connecting frequencies of each energy form providing an interface to allow the influence of the higher energy form to connect with the next lower energy form, until eventually reaching the physical form, which we are able to recognise through the narrow spectrum of our own senses.

Gerber's text provides an extraordinary level of detailed explanation and reasoning behind the existence of a wide range of vibrational realms that impact our health and well-being.

Cyndi Dale provides a similar explanation to Richard Gerber. She quotes the work of Stanford Professor William Tiller. Dr Tiller describes himself as a "card-carrying scientist" who meditates and is interested in subtle energies. He says that since the 1970s, he has developed an "inside university life" of conventional science at Stanford University and an "outside university life" of psychoenergetics.[37]

Dr Tiller talks about the "conditioning of a space" with a particular intention. In the 1990s, he conducted four experiments with the hypothesis that the accepted scientific assumption formed by Descartes in the 1600s was no longer relevant in today's world. In Dr Tiller's words, that assumption was "that no human qualities of consciousness, intention, emotion, mind or spirit can significantly influence a well-designed targeted experiment in physical reality." His view is that this assumption continues to exist today within orthodox science and orthodox medicine.

Dr Tiller conducted four target experiments:

1. Increase the pH of water by one full pH unit through intention with no chemical additions.

2. Take the same water and decrease the pH by one full pH unit through intention with no chemical additions.

3. Take a specific liver enzyme and place it in a conditioned space with the intention to significantly increase the chemical activity by a thirty-minute exposure to that conditioned space.

4. Take an example of a living system, fruit fly larvae, and change its molecular makeup from two phosphorous atoms in the molecule to three phosphorous atoms in the molecule. The outcome would be to make the fruit fly larvae more

physically fit and therefore shorten the larval development time to the adult fly stage.

To conduct these experiments, Dr Tiller found a way to imprint an intention into a simple electrical device from a deep meditative state. When this happened, not only would it change the physical properties of things but also the physical reality of the space, which becomes conditioned to this intention.

All four experiments were robustly successful and unequivocally proved that the basic assumption of Descartes no longer held in today's world.

Despite the clear outcome of these controlled scientific experiments, Dr Tiller notes that the medical and scientific communities are not interested in "looking down the microscope," drawing an analogy with Galileo, whose work with the telescope proved Copernicus's theory that the sun, not the earth, was the centre of the universe. Dr Tiller concedes that eventually acceptance did occur. His explanation for this delayed acceptance is that there is always a long lag time from one paradigm to another.

One of the reasons he says that these concepts will eventually be accepted is because of the very nature of the concepts themselves. The general public is fascinated with these types of discoveries. Many people have experienced these concepts, even if only as moments of connection with others—knowing what they were thinking or knowing who is on the other end of the phone before they pick up the phone. Ironically, Dr Tiller points out, as more and more people develop this belief, there will develop a greater level of connectivity between people. As a result, the space will become filled with this intention, and it will increase the uptake by the scientific community themselves—a self-fulfilling prophecy in many ways.

Dr Tiller's more recent work has been with the use of intention to impact the physical well-being of humans by broadcasting that intention across great distances. From a healing perspective, he conducted successful experiments with people suffering from depression, located all around the world. In order to allow the sustained focus and intention over a long period of time, he used the electrical device that had been imprinted with the intention and continuously fed the names and addresses of the individuals into the computer system. Dr Tiller draws the same conclusions as the Institute of HeartMath, that the intention can only be maintained when the person is in a state of coherence. As it is very difficult for any human to maintain coherence at this level for a long period of time, he chose to imprint the intention into the electrical device in order for his experiments to have a valid foundation.

Over time, Dr Tiller has developed his own view of the levels of subtle energy in the universe. It is this work that Cyndi Dale refers to in her text. Dr Tiller has defined six main levels, with some sublevels, starting with the physical and concluding with the divine. Dr MacManaway operates through the prism of a shamanic map with seven levels, also starting with the physical and concluding with the upper spiritual. As modern man is only now starting to explore these other levels of consciousness, it is not surprising that there may be some discrepancy in how many levels exist beyond the physical world. Where there is no difference of opinion is that Dr

Tiller, Dr MacManaway, Cyndi Dale, and Dr Gerber all agree that in order to communicate into the etheric level and above, we must move beyond our five senses at least to our sixth sense, our intuition. It is this intuition and its capacity to communicate with the various types of subtle energy that is so important when wrapping your head around the concepts of vibrational healing.

Cyndi Dale describes vibrational medicine as "the intentional use of a frequency to positively affect another frequency or to bring an organism into balance."[42] Specifically with respect to sound healing, Cyndi Dale describes it as a "vibrational therapy that impacts all levels of the human self—as well as all living organisms."[38] She emphasises that one of the most important aspects of sound is the state of entrainment that occurs when several different objects or systems vibrate or resonate together. "When the body entrains to positive thoughts, such as faith, hope, and love, studies show that overall health improves."[39] Conversely, when the body resonates to negative thoughts, some type of discord will eventuate, creating a lack of ease, or dis-ease. Cyndi Dale goes on to explain that every human being generates his or her own harmonic or vibratory range that is particular to the self. She says that living beings will pick up on frequencies that vibrate within their particular range and resist the ones that do not.[40]

Sound therapists, according to Cyndi Dale, ultimately diagnose or determine invading frequencies and then determine which other frequencies will eliminate the invading force or strengthen the person's natural frequencies. She also suggests that the two opposing frequencies can be attuned to work together in a healthy way. Later I will describe my own experiences with sound therapy.

In the following chapters, it is assumed that you hold at least some belief in the ideas and concepts put forward so far and that possibly, just possibly, at least some of these concepts might be a potentially powerful force and natural healing tool in our lives.

If I have provided you with at least a sliver of explanation to which you can relate, then you will find inspiring possibilities when you read on.

As my personal interest and inquiry has continued into the ethereal and its possibilities, I have found myself learning and witnessing that these principles of vibrational medicine apply not only to the human body but also to animals. In addition, they apply equally to our ability to influence the landscape and to reconnect with its natural rhythms. Vibrational medicine shows us that when we learn to listen to the messages from our body about its own energy flow, we can use our intent and tools to assist in strengthening that energetic framework, which then makes possible the physical or organic healing that follows. That same skill of learning to listen to the messages from our body is also available to us to listen to the energetic messages in the landscape. Practitioners of natural healing of the human body draw on many different aspects of vibrational medicine to aid their craft. Equally, practitioners of natural healing of the landscape also draw on their knowledge of those same energetic influences with an intent directed towards the healing of the natural rhythms in the landscape, as distinct from the natural rhythms in the human body.

I believe now that they are not distinct and separate at all.

Dr Patrick MacManaway has dedicated much of the past decade applying his energetic healing skills to the landscape, particularly working with farmers who no longer follow the industrialised farming model and now embrace a range of different natural farming systems. This energetic healing of the landscape is known as geomancy. Dr MacManaway's work is conducted in the UK, the United States, and Australia. It is interesting to note that whilst these three countries demonstrate some of the poorest nutritional density in their foods and also apply the industrialised agricultural model extensively throughout their farming landscape, they are the same countries where serious questions are now being asked by farmers who can see for themselves the decline in their landscape health.

Dr MacManaway works with vegetable growers, dairy farmers, grain farmers, as well as sheep and cattle farmers. His work ranges from improving the water quality in the troughs and dams for the livestock to reducing mastitis in dairy herds, improving germination with vegetable seeds, reducing insect infestations in grain farms, and improving the energy in animal-handling facilities.

Whilst Dr MacManaway is very practiced and experienced in his work, he is not alone in these types of pursuits in the agricultural communities of our western countries. Increasingly, farmers who accept the principles behind vibrational healing are also learning the skills and adopting these practices for themselves. Many of their counterparts in non-industrialised farming communities would have learnt these skills from their parents and grandparents. Returning to the power of their intuition and an acceptance of the ability of humans to connect with nature's rhythms—human, animal, plant, and landscape—shows us that possibilities do exist to seriously consider alternatives to reductionist, linear models of food production. These "new" models allow us to enhance the natural farming systems and strengthen their connection with the landscape from which they draw. In the ensuing decades, we will see an expansion of these practices as more individuals make their own choices of how to balance the landscapes with which they work. As more questions are asked and more people see and experience these new possibilities, the paradigms will have to change.

For people who connect with the land, the experience is very real. The sense of loss that is felt by families who have lived and worked their whole lives on a particular landscape is itself a loss of energetic connection. Indigenous cultures consistently speak of this connection. In our family's case, we knew that the grandmother in our family was intimately connected with both the landscape and her cattle. We knew that. We accepted it. We couldn't have explained it like I can explain it now. Such is the case for many people who rely on their land to produce its bounty as a result of its natural ebbs and flows.

Chapter 8

Vibrational Medicine—My Family's Experience

Although we were farmers, my earliest experiences with vibrational healing were not to do with the landscape. They came about because of my inquisitiveness towards alternatives for human health. The parallels between landscape healing and human healing seem obvious to me now.

Then, it seemed almost like another world hearing about the power of intent and vibrations as healing tools for the human body. For many years, I had been developing an increasing awareness of all things being connected somehow, and this awareness was enhanced through a number of credible accounts from friends and colleagues about subtle energy as a mode of healing for people. Perhaps not coincidentally, these friends and colleagues were also part of the Australian farming community and practicing a range of different natural farming systems. For these particular farmers, the leap from their experience with subtle energy for human health to subtle energy for their landscapes was almost seamless. Some of those farmers are today expanding their landscape knowledge further and working directly with Dr MacManaway and other geomancy practitioners.

I came to know this group of pioneers as part of the farming network that has been built on the back of the very strong landscape vision held by Terry McCosker for more than twenty-five years. These farmers had moved away from the desire to dominate and returned to a listening mode of operation. On reflection now, I believe they use both the universal intelligence of the heart and the individual intellect of the brain, as Joseph Chilton Pearce describes it. From these credible conversations and explanations, as well as my own increasing awareness, I came to accept the possibility that healing could perhaps occur at this vibrational level.

Having accepted vibrational healing as a possibility, the time came when our family had the choice to experience one form of this healing modality. I will relay two incidents that helped secure my belief that we had been part of an experience that we would not previously have considered possible. The modality of vibrational healing that I have come to understand and practice as a healing practitioner has been called vibrational kinesiology, specifically known as the Dawson Program—so named after its founder, an Australian by the name of Cameron Dawson. I will explain its history and principles in due course. First I will relay these two stories to set the scene for my piqued curiosity and subsequent further study.

These experiences happened to members of my extended family and not to me personally. Whilst I have had many positive experiences from different vibrational healing methodologies, my responses to this healing were more gradual in their impact and so not as easily described or profound in their singular reaction.

One person in our extended family, we will call Felicity, had experienced difficulties throughout her schooling with reading, writing, and comprehension. By contrast, her mathematical and social skills were very high. She played musical instruments for many years and participated in a wide range of sporting activities. In middle high school years, Felicity was assessed by a child psychologist as having a reading level five years below her age. She was also diagnosed with a form of dyslexia, which manifested itself in her inability to track words any further than the midline of a page, with some letters appearing in a jumbled order. For Felicity, each word had to be read individually before she could move onto the next word. By the time she had completed all the words in a line or a sentence, she could no longer remember what the sentence was about. Such difficulties meant that her tested written comprehension levels were also very low.

To assist Felicity, the school system provided her with a range of supportive mechanisms, including someone to be a reader for her school examinations so that she could listen to the questions rather than have to read them herself. In addition, she was given extended time to answer the questions and the use of a keyboard so that she could type the answers rather than having to form the letters with her hands. She also had the constant support of a tutor who used special techniques to draw out her academic ability and ensure that it was represented in her assessment. Felicity's own attitude was very positive, and her teacher's engagement with her remained strong, enhanced by her strong social skills and endearing personality. Felicity had always loved history but acknowledged that she would not be able to do these subjects because of the immense quantity of reading required. Importantly, she had read only one book in all her high school years. This was a short murder-mystery book based on a true story.

With a combination of these support mechanisms and Felicity's own commitment, she was successful at enrolling in university. Her first two years of study were extremely difficult. Her mother has often said that she simultaneously completed the same study course as she provided so much support and assistance to Felicity during this time!

These circumstances were presented to the practitioner of the Dawson Program. His explanation was simple and yet extraordinary. He was able to ascertain that Felicity had experienced a physical trauma at birth (subsequently identified as being a forceps delivery). This physical trauma had placed pressure on the cranial bones and caused an energetic blockage, which stopped those cranial bones from realigning as part of the natural process after birth. This blockage, he said, had then caused her cranial bones to stay in a minutely misaligned position, putting pressure on her brain and causing a misfiring of the pathways between the left and right hemispheres. This caused images to be distorted to her vision and made tracking across the page difficult for her eyes to achieve. As his explanation unfolded, it made perfect sense that misaligned cranial bones could cause such side effects. Her parents didn't really understand how a vibrational healing correction could make a difference, but they felt that if the possibility was there, then this was the opportunity to see if it could make a difference, however small.

Once this energetic correction had occurred, the practitioner then explained that whilst the energetic flow had been rebalanced, it would take some time for the physical body to catch up, and for the synapses that had not previously been able to connect to build those connections. He explained that the energetic conditions had been set for the body to now undertake its physical healing process, but it would take time, perhaps even six to twelve months. He conducted one more energetic correction about six weeks later as a normal follow-up procedure.

Around six months later, Felicity was taking an overseas working holiday and surprised herself when she felt compelled to purchase some word-search books to use on the plane. On her return, over the coming months, she gradually started reading books, and by the end of the twelve-month period, she was reading two or three books at a time! It was as though she had so much to catch up on. She began reading a range of personal development/self-help books. She was able to demonstrate her comprehension by discussing in detail the concepts in these books and their potential application to her own life. This process demonstrated a very high level of comprehension—to be able to understand what she had read and then to be able to reflect on that information in sufficient detail to then apply it to her own circumstances. Such comprehension from written material had not been possible for Felicity just one year earlier. She also started reading historic accounts of Australians in prisoner-of-war camps, fulfilling part of her long-held interest in history. After a time, she made the choice that these were not uplifting in her life, so she swapped to other fiction and nonfiction genres.

Felicity completed her university degree and progressed into the workforce. Subsequently, she changed her career interests and found herself enrolling in a diploma to pursue additional study. This time the study was completely online. Such a decision may not have been possible earlier in her life, as her reading and comprehension required so much verbal assistance. In this online study, there was absolutely no teacher/student face-to-face contact to allow discussion of the class content and assessment material. This contrasted starkly with her previous learning environments, which had relied very heavily on group learning and student-teacher discussions to aid her learning. It was possible for her to make a phone appointment with a tutor if required. Most assessment was undertaken using written material. Throughout the course, Felicity achieved results similar to a distinction level in the grading system!

This is a remarkable transformation in someone's life. It is particularly remarkable because I am aware that Felicity's family's search for answers had led them to a range of different diagnoses throughout her primary and secondary schooling. Each diagnosis led to particular support activities to assist her with her reading and comprehension. Many of these activities had given her small improvements, often not long lasting unless the activity was continued. None had given her the results that this energetic healing provided. I found it so remarkable that I decided I would pursue this vibrational healing modality. As I mentioned, the modality is classified as a form of vibrational kinesiology and it is known as the Dawson Program. As part of that process, I attached myself as a student to the practitioner who had conducted the correction with Felicity. Whenever possible, I participated with him in the energetic healing process, while simultaneously learning the background and underlying principles to vibrational healing.

While I was engaged in this student role, another member of our extended family, whom I will call Max, volunteered to participate and requested an energetic correction of his own. The correction took about two hours. The practitioner explained that for some people the correction can precipitate a body cleanse. This may be a headache, sudden tiredness, emotional vulnerability, skin irritation, or loose bowel motions—similar to the symptoms of other body cleanses. Immediately after Max received the energetic correction, he went to the toilet. He returned minutes later exclaiming that his urine was virtually black! While Max couldn't really understand or explain the energetic process he had just experienced, he was certain of what he had just seen!

And so my direct, personal learning in this fascinating world of vibrational healing had begun. I am now a practitioner and teacher in this simple yet profound discipline.

The Dawson Program Explained

"The Dawson program views the human body as a naturally self-creating, self-correcting system when given the opportunity to be so."[41]

The Dawson Program synthesises ancient practices from different cultures, drawing together different energetic frameworks and packaging them in a way that it can be understood through the intellect of our head and felt through the intelligence of our heart. It operates with thirty-two basic precepts, some of which will now be discussed.

There are four steps to the healing process in the Dawson Program. They are simple. They require a humble state of grace, a trust in nature, a trust in one's ability to connect with someone else, as well as an acceptance of the power of vibrations on the human body.

1. The first step in the healing process is the patient's subconscious permission for the assessment and healing to occur. Belief in the healing process has been widely discussed already. In the Dawson Program, this buy-in is at a subconscious level.

2. The second aspect is the intent of the healer to make a connection with the patient to allow the assessment and healing to occur. A perspective on this aspect of the healing process can be understood by referring back to the explanations given earlier in the book from the work of the Institute of HeartMath, Cleve Backster, Dr William Tiller, and the writings of Greg Bradden,

when they highlight that focus and intent provide the environment to allow the heart to make energetic connections with other people and thus influence the rhythm of the body's systems.

3. The third aspect is a disciplined investigative process, which follows a strict protocol. This investigative process allows the practitioner to identify three separate elements to the healing equation. The first is the identification of the energetic system that requires correction. The second is the source or cause of that imbalance. This could be either a physical trauma, a toxicity in the body, or an unresolved emotional issue. The third aspect of the investigation is identifying the particular frequencies that can be used to affect the energetic correction, which then allows the physical body to begin its own healing process. This investigative methodology taps into the body's subconscious innate responses. As this methodology has not previously been discussed in this book, I will provide a more detailed explanation here.

This methodology allows the practitioner to ask questions of the body that the person could not necessarily answer with his or her conscious mind. The focused mind of the practitioner and the permission of the patient allow questions to be asked either verbally or silently. The questions are asked following a logical and detailed protocol, with each question framed for a binary response of either yes or no. The body's subconscious response to these questions is provided with one of two potential muscle responses. Following this binary questioning protocol allows the practitioner to systematically use these responses to work through a flow chart of questions, eliminating possibilities until he identifies the issue that needs to be dealt with as well as the tools required for the healing to occur.

Such a testing technique is now commonly called muscle testing. George Goodheart, a chiropractor in the United States in the 1960s, developed this technique for modern practice. He gave it the term "applied kinesiology," referring to the application of the muscles' responses as a tool to help identify the part of the body requiring treatment. Many natural therapists and some orthodox practitioners have since adopted this technique to assist in their diagnoses.

Psychiatrist Dr John Diamond has studied extensively the use of this muscle-testing technique as a valid methodology to determine answers of yes and no to binary questions relating to the human body. This research has been published in his book *Your Body Doesn't Lie.*

To assist in the explanation, it might be helpful to highlight that water diviners apply this same technique in a slightly different way. They use a binary questioning process to help determine the presence, quality, depth, and flow of water in the landscape. Rather than using another person's muscle response, they use their own muscles' response to the energetic flow of the landscape. As they ask a particular question, the divining rods move in one of two possible directions until eventually the diviner comes to a point where he believes he has gathered all the answers required.

4. Having made the connection between patient and practitioner and identified the necessary information, the fourth step in this process is the use of a range of vibrational healing frequencies. These healing frequencies are mainly sound frequencies. The playing of these frequencies aids in the release of energy, allowing it to unblock and to flow again. In addition to sound frequencies, the Dawson Program also uses colour frequencies and crystal frequencies, as well as affirmations, which express their own frequencies through the energy of thought and the spoken word.

Perhaps the simplest explanation of the work of the Dawson Program is that it accesses the power of intention and the use of frequencies to correct the energetic flow of energy through and around the body to allow the body to self-heal.

The Dawson Program draws on many of the principles discussed in this book so far. It "differs from the conventional Western medical approach to human and animal physical construction, health and illness."[41] This different approach is detailed in the thirty-two precepts of the Dawson Program.

At the outset, the first two precepts of the Dawson Program align with Richard Gerber. Precept number one states: "Human and animal bodies are constructed on an electrical framework called the Meridian System. This framework is found in each of the follicles of the ovaries of each female child or young animal at birth." It goes on to say that "the meridian system has been called many different names, such as framework, matrix, hologram and etheric body."[41]

Precept number two follows on with "This framework is formed around a basic gradient of energy found in all seeds, human and animal ovarian follicles."[41] The Dawson Program uses the Sanskrit word Kundalini to name this gradient of energy. This can be equated with the work done by Burr with his gradients of energy identified in the salamander and the sprouted seed, which led him to the conclusion that "Any developing organism was destined to follow a prescribed growth template and that such a template was generated by the organism's individual electromagnetic field."[34]

Regarding the importance of this electrical framework, precept number twenty states, in part, "The source of illness in the human body is a combination of frequency malfunctions and water and nutrient deficiency, which can be further exacerbated by chemical damage ..."[41]

As quoted earlier from Gerber, "The physical body is so energetically connected and dependent upon the etheric body for cellular guidance that the physical body cannot exist without the etheric body. If the etheric field becomes distorted, physical disease soon follows."[36]

Bruce Lipton's major contribution to modern science so far has been his unravelling of how our thoughts, experiences, and environment influence our DNA, thus concluding that we are not at the mercy of our DNA and have the power and capacity to influence it continually throughout our lives.

Precept three, four, and seven of the Dawson Program give detailed explanations of the role of the DNA. Precept three states: "Following conception, the DNA in the first cell becomes immediately a new thinking creature in its own right and takes control over the meridian framework as its basis for the construction of its own body." Precept four goes on to say (in part): "The DNA is in itself a mind. It enlarges the meridian framework as it constructs extra cells …" Precept seven follows on, "In the DNA of the new cell there are special genes which create specific electrical fields known in the Dawson Program system as Shape Fields whose function is to create the individual shape and sex for the new body and give form and position to each organ and each portion of anatomy, however minute. These Shape Fields form around the meridian framework."[41]

Bruce Lipton emphasises that our DNA both affects and is affected by our physical and emotional health and well-being. Similarly, the Dawson Program believes that electrical fields both affect and are affected by the DNA. Precept eight states (in part) that "All life forms have energy within their cells which function at an exact frequency. This 'Life Force' is created … as a response to the commands of the DNA and energises the … electrical systems of the new body and thereby each group of organs including skin, bone, blood etc."[45] The concept of life force is very important in the Dawson Program as the role of the energy systems is to maximise the life force of every cell in the human body. Interruption to the energy flow of any of the particular energy systems can reduce the life force of cells, organs, and physiological systems, resulting in a minor or major imbalance in the body.

When referring to the body's electrical framework, the Dawson Program recognises twenty-eight main electrical frequencies: fourteen meridians, seven chakras, and seven auric fields. Precept sixteen describes what can affect each of these energetic systems. "Each of these systems has individual frequencies which can be affected by shock, thus causing an imbalance in the triad of health …" The shock can be from a physical interference (for example, a fall or a car accident), a toxic interference (something ingested that poisons the body), or from an emotional interference (some negative disturbance to our thoughts or feelings that remains unhealed). "The most powerful long-term effect on the human being is the effect on our emotions which have chain reactions throughout our chemical and physical make-up."[41]

Precept seventeen goes on to say (in part), "If any of the 28 cardinal frequencies are altered … the sub-conscious mind will use the body's own muscles and bone structure to re-align the physical structure to this now imperfect framework. If this is not corrected, illness will follow ..."

The consequence of this warped framework is detailed in precept eighteen: "If the matrix remains in an altered state, the body remains permanently in a warped condition until corrected."[41]

Energetic Systems of the Dawson Program

As identified earlier, the three energetic systems incorporated in the Dawson Program are the twenty-eight cardinal frequencies that emanate from seven auric fields, seven chakras, and fourteen meridians. These three energetic systems have been known to ancient cultures for thousands of years.

Auric Fields

Auric fields have been used mostly by the Tibetan culture. In the Dawson Program, our individual auric fields are recognised as our detectors and protectors. The first auric field is called the Kundalini. It represents the gradient of energy found in the ovarian follicles and around which the entire human electrical framework is then formed. The energy from the Kundalini flows up the spine. The six other auric fields form at the moment of first breath. They surround our body externally and connect us to the energies of the universe. When functioning well, they inform our subconscious of the influences of our external world. This includes being aware that someone is staring at you, walking on rough surfaces without tripping, as well as knowing when someone is going to contact you. When these auric fields are not functioning well, you may be prone to accidents, feel disconnected with the world around you, or even feel uncomfortable with physical contact, among other things. "Auric fields can be altered by shock, causing malfunction, creating extreme anxiety and major behavioural problems, affecting both chakra and meridian function and frequency."[42]

Chakras

The study and practice of chakra energy healing has been part of Indian culture, particularly Hindu tradition, for thousands of years. Chakras are more widely understood than auric fields and have been extensively studied and frequently included in a range of healing disciplines that are practiced in western countries.

In the Dawson Program, the seven major chakras energise the body from the moment of conception. The chakras are positioned along the body from the crown of the skull to the base of the spine. Diagrams of chakras generally show a colour range of the rainbow. There is a reason for this. As explained by Cameron Dawson, energy created by the chakras has frequencies that are harmonics of white light. (The colours of the rainbow are also white light. They are segregated into component colours by raindrops acting as prisms.) There are seven chakras just as there are seven separate colour segments comprising white light. The frequency of the base chakra is an harmonic of the base colour of the spectrum—red, the second from red being orange, then yellow, green, light blue, dark blue, through to purple, which is the crown chakra—the frequency of which is an harmonic for the colour purple. Chakras create energy to supply the meridians and the auric fields. Each of the chakra entry points is related to individual glands and organs. "The crown chakra connects to the pineal [gland], the anterior brow chakra to the pituitary, the throat chakra to the thyroid, the heart chakra to the heart, the solar plexus to the small intestine, the reproduction chakra to reproductive organs and the base chakra to the coccyx or base of the spine ..."[43] The energy taken in by the chakras is used and then dissipated, relieved, balanced, and exits the body by the twenty-eight minor chakras. Malfunctioning chakras can show up as a range of physical ailments, including a weakened heart, as well as emotional limitations such as a lack of self-worth, a sense of not feeling grounded in life, or an inability to speak your mind. "While chakras function, there is life. When the chakras cease to function, the life force ceases and, therefore, life ceases."[44]

"Life force is a complicated concept, not incorporated in western medical notions of anatomy, physiology and function. Although not specifically recognised by our scientific community, life force is an integral variable measurable force as important to human and animal function as oxygen water and nutrients."[45]

Meridians

The meridian energy system is the third of the energy systems embraced in the Dawson Program. In modern historic times, the meridian system has been recognised and understood extensively through the ancient Chinese discipline of acupuncture, which is now widely practiced across the world. In the Dawson Program, the meridians are recognised as the framework on which the physical body is formed. "Meridians are the basic matrix/hologram/ electrical framework that forms the fundamental structure of all plant and animal life."[40] It is the meridians that power each and every cell in our bodies, receiving their energy from the chakras at conception. As precept eighteen states, "If the matrix remains in an altered state, the body remains permanently in a warped condition until corrected."[41] Each of the fourteen meridians that form the matrix has its own specific frequency created from the base chakra frequency.

In addition to having serious impact on our physical form, the fourteen major meridians are also associated with our major emotions, including our levels of tolerance and degrees of happiness, faith, love, security, self-worth, generosity, forgiveness, contentment, joy, and inner harmony. Psychiatrist Dr John Diamond, in his book *Life Energy*, details these meridians and their associated emotions. The positive affirmations that Dr John Diamond developed are incorporated into the Dawson Program as the affirmations associated with the emotional correction of each meridian. Malfunctioning meridians will generally have an associated negative emotion. A positive affirmation helps to build the energy flow of that meridian. In addition to these affirmations, the Dawson Program also uses a range of instrument frequencies, as well as specific crystals that resonate with the frequencies of the meridians.

Cam Dawson's extensive study of these practices incorporated not only the observations and beliefs relating to the functions of the human body but also the appropriate sound frequencies that relate to each of these twenty-eight different energetic frequencies.

This simple discipline allows the practitioner to connect with the whole person and facilitate that person's inner healing. Searching through the complexity to find the simplicity is one of life's great challenges when we work from our intellect. Simplicity often comes to us when we connect with our heart. The Dawson Program is one such example. Operating from fundamental principles of nature, as the practitioner moves into a state of grace, it seems that the energy emanating from the heart connects with the heart of the patient and allows for the flow of information not otherwise available to the conscious mind.

Simple Yet Profound

As I have previously described, depending on the correction, the patient can experience quite a significant physical change. On other occasions, the patient will experience an overwhelming sense of lightness, having released a great deal of emotional blockage, often built up over a long period of time, sometimes carried from previous generations. This often involves an emotional response and a sense of relief that is associated with this newfound feeling.

So much of what the Dawson Program represents is on its way to being explained by modern science, albeit in a very disjointed way. It appears that Cameron Dawson was a truly extraordinary individual to have committed himself for more than thirty years to the research and practice of vibrational healing, culminating in this discipline that encompasses so much about the human spirit and our physical and emotional well-being.

We often hear the challenge when new concepts surface in our world: "Prove it." I recently heard a response that seems appropriate here: "Try it."

The Dawson Program is just one form of vibrational medicine. Many of its principles are a revelation to modern science, albeit ancient in their origins. Some of its principles really do require you to trust in order for the healing to deliver the best possible results. This, in itself, can be difficult to accept when we have become so used to tangible, linear approaches to our healing practices.

This notion takes us right back to an acceptance that the whole is often greater than the sum of its parts. For the Dawson Program and vibrational medicine in general, this is undoubtedly the case. For man's life on earth to advance at the same time as we also aim to heal the planet, I believe this shift in perspective will gain momentum. As Dr William Tiller predicts, as the consciousness of individuals shifts, then the space surrounding us will also be filled, allowing more people, including our scientific communities, to embrace these age-old questions now dressed up in modern clothing.

We can look forward to exciting and challenging times ahead as the chasm between these different belief systems narrows, and we move closer to connecting and benefiting from the rhythms of nature that are available to us, and hopefully a greater capacity to explain and define that which to many is, at the moment, indefinable.

Conclusion

Life is a series of experiences. Perhaps you believe there are reasons for these experiences. I do. I believe there has been a purpose to my life's journey to this point. Joining the dots on seemingly disconnected concepts has created a new prism through which I now view the world.

It is a prism of infinite possibilities, powered by nature and guided by humans through the frequencies of love, appreciation, and forgiveness.

Through this new prism, I often look back on the fifty years of our farming family and realise how far we have all come. I also wonder how far we have yet to travel.

Our farm is sold, and we've carved new lives. We've also found a new rhythm to live our lives. It's a gentler rhythm and much less judgemental. We reaped many rewards from that time and also brought with us a great deal of pain. We are still healing from that pain. For different members of our three generations, it's a different type of healing. The sense of loss that some experienced has now eased. The sense of connection that we feel again as a family helps greatly. From being a father, so distant and yet so committed, for Bill it's a powerful new place to be so engaged in all our family interactions. That connection allows for powerful reflection and powerful healing. From each of us previously feeling alone and isolated, we've moved to a softer, kinder way. It's uplifting to be part of. From being a mother, steeped in an unexpressed anxiety about our lives and how they were going to play out, I now revel in the challenges and opportunities that life provides, immensely grateful to have been able to commit time to exploring and learning, and also to writing this book. Scars still exist for all of us. But just as the earth's soil has the capacity to regenerate, so too does the human body, emotionally and physically. I'm convinced of the potency of love, appreciation, and forgiveness. I forget them frequently and have to remind myself to revisit their strength.

We actively use food as a healing tool, and we actively use our knowledge of vibrational healing to help to rebalance the energetic framework of our bodies. Part of that healing has been to reduce the toxic overload in Bill's body from the two decades of chemicals he was exposed to. Part of it is also the release of emotional blockages that also built up for our family members during that time. We recognise such experiences are part of life and have become part of our rich learning ground. We are grateful to have found some tools to progress beyond our pain and sadness.

For the grandparents who pioneered many aspects of our business on the back of so much blood, sweat, and tears, they remain an inspiration to this day. They acknowledge, with so much gratitude, the rewards they have received from their lives; and they accept, without judgement or resentment, the challenges that have ailed them at different times. Even now, in their eighties, they pop a bottle of sparkling wine each year for their wedding anniversary and for New Year's Eve and thank each other for the lives they have led. For the grandchildren, our children, they will probably never know farming life as adults. That opportunity has probably passed them by, and that's okay. As they explore different opportunities in the world, we hope that they will retain fond memories of their childhoods and recognise that our livelihood as we knew it was not sustainable for us or for our land.

I reflect on the frequencies that surround us, pulse through us, and indeed are us. I marvel at how the physical structure of the human body parallels the physical structure of the soil on earth. I marvel at the synergy that flows when we allow that soil to engage in its natural cycles, enhancing its resonance with healing frequencies, then ultimately providing us with nature's bounties to feed our bodies with food as nature intended.

I wonder what paths modern science is going to take as it applies its intellect to prove what the heart already knows … and wonder when our societies will reach a point of acceptance and release, then return to the heart to seek our direction.

> *Whatever the journey, whatever the time frame, we can each advance as individuals, and combined we will also advance the consciousness of human life at the same time as advancing the health of our planet.*

Final Note

I know that my journey is just one. I also know that it is incomplete and will always be incomplete. These are my personal stories. This is my personal journey of inquiry. And this is my knowledge that I have gained so far along the way. I believe it is worth sharing, and I hope to tip the scales of inquiry for others who read this book.

My answers are not your answers. We are each responsible for our own lives. Taking back that personal responsibility, listening to your own body, and making your own informed choices will allow you to find your own answers.

Please share your journey and your answers with me.

I would like to hear your stories and how you have joined dots in your own life to make a change for the better—for you, for your family, and for life on earth.

Please visit my website www.margaretbridgeford. com.au for resources you may find helpful to extend your knowledge about concepts I have introduced in this book.

With love, appreciation and forgiveness,

Margaret Bridgeford

Illustrations

1. "About Chronic Disease," *National Health Council* (29 July 2014), Web, 17 Nov. 2014.
2. "National Chronic Diseases Strategy," *Australian Government Department of Health and Ageing* (1 Jan. 2006), Web, 10 Oct. 2014.
3. Yang, Yang, "Trends in US Adult Chronic Disease Mortality, 1960–1999: Age, Period and Cohort Variations," *US National Library of Medicine National Institute of Health* (1 May 2008), Web, 17 Nov. 2014.
4. "Population Estimates | Ecology Global Network," Ecology Global Network (21 Sept. 2011), Web, 6 Jan. 2015. <http://www.ecology.com/population-estimates-year-2050/>.
5. "Fertilizer Consumption and Grain Production for the World, 1950–2013," Earth Policy Institute (8 Jan. 2014), Web, 6 Jan. 2015. <http://www.earth-policy.org/data_center/C24>.
6. R.C. Dalal, W.M. Strong, E.J. Weston, and J. Gaffney, "Sustaining Multiple Production Systems. Soil Fertility Decline and Restoration of Cropping Lands in Sub Tropical Queensland," *Tropical Grasslands* 25 (1991): 173–80. Print.

7.   Robert Alexander McCance and Elsie May Widdowson, *McCance and Widdowson's: The Composition of Foods: Sixth Summary Edition* 06, 6th Summary ed. (Cambridge: Royal Society of Chemistry, 2002). Print.

8.   David Thomas, "A Study on the Mineral Depletion of Foods Available to Us as a Nation over the Period 1940 to 1991," *Mineral Resources International (UK) Ltd.* (1 Jan. 2000), Web, 24 Nov. 2014.

9.   "Electromagnetic Spectrum Diagram," *MY NASA DATA*. National Aeronautics and Space Administration, Web, 2 Dec. 2014.

10. Institute of HeartMath, 1997.

11. Manfred Clynes.

12. Institute of HeartMath, 2009.

13. Photographs Office Masaru Emoto, LLC.

Endnotes

1. Michael Pollan, *The Omnivore's Dilemma: The Search for a Perfect Meal in a Fast-food World* (London: Bloomsbury, 2007).

2. J. Trappe, "A.B. Frank and Mycorrhizae: The Challenge to Evolu ... [Mycorrhiza. 2005]—PubMed Result," *National Center for Biotechnology Information*, Web, 10 July 2011.

3. Lady Eve Balfour, *The Living Soil* (Soil Association, 2006), 46.

4. Ibid., 48.

5. *Principles of Healthy Diets* (Washington DC: Weston A Price Foundation, 2010).

6. Sally Fallon and Mary G. Enig, *Nourishing Traditions: The Cookbook That Challenges Politically Correct Nutrition and the Diet Dictocrats*, Rev. 2nd ed., (Washington, DC: NewTrends Pub., 2001), 12.

7. Sir Albert Howard, "Introduction." *An Agricultural Testament* (London: Oxford UP, 1943).

8. Stefan Mager, *Permaculture Guide* (Mullumbimby, N.S.W.: Aracariaguides).

9. Brian Keats and Stefan Mager, *Biodynamic Growing: Healthcare for Earth and Humanity*, 2nd Extended ed. (Mullumbimby, N.S.W.: Aracariaguides, 2009).

10. Norman Cousins, *Anatomy of an Illness as Perceived by the Patient* (New York: WW Norton, 2005), 18.

11. Ibid., 49.

12. Rachael Moeller, "Study Suggests Common Knee Surgery's Effect Is Purely Placebo," *Scientific American Global RSS* (12 July 2002), Web, 5 Sept. 2014.

13. Norman Cousins, *Anatomy of an Illness as Perceived by the Patient* (New York: WW Norton, 2005), 64.

14. Ibid., 76.

15. Ibid., 149.

16. Ibid., 151.

17. Bruce Lipton, *The Biology of Belief*, 12th ed. (New York: Hay House, 2010), 155.

18. Ibid., 37.

19. Ibid., 31.

20. S. L. Berger, T. Kouzarides, R. Shiekhattar, and A. Shilatifard, "An Operational Definition Of Epigenetics," *Genes & Development*, 781–83.

21. Cyndi Dale, *The Subtle Body: An Encyclopedia of Your Energetic Anatomy* (Boulder, Colo.: Sounds True, 2009), 43.

22. Bruce Lipton, *The Biology of Belief*, 12th ed. (New York: Hay House, 2010), 39.

23. Cyndi Dale, *The Subtle Body: An Encyclopedia of Your Energetic Anatomy* (Boulder, Colo.: Sounds True, 2009), 42.

24. Michael Toms, *Heart Intelligence*, Dimensions Radio Network, 19 June 2011, Radio.

25. Richard Gerber, *Vibrational Medicine: The #1 Handbook of Subtle-energy Therapies*, 3rd ed. (Rochester, VT: Bear, 2001), 22.

26. *Solar Revolution*, Perf. Dieter Broers, Richard Sheldrake, Screen Addiction, 2012. DVD.

27. Rolin McCraty, Mike Atkinson, Dana Tomasino, and Raymond Bradley, *The Coherent Heart* (Boulder: Institute of HeartMath, 2006), 24.

28. Cyndi Dale, *The Subtle Body: An Encyclopedia of Your Energetic Anatomy* (Boulder, Colo.: Sounds True, 2009), 67.

29. Doc Lew Childre and Mike Atkinson, *Science of the Heart: Exploring the Role of the Heart* (Boulder Creek, CA: HeartMath Research Center, Institute of HearMath, 2001), 20–21.

30. Ibid., 8.

31. Cleve Backster, *Primary Perception: Biocommunication with Plants, Living Foods and Human Cells* (Anza, CA: White Rose Millennium, 2003), 105.

32. *The Language of the Divine Matrix*, distributed by Source Books, Inc., 2007. Film.

33. Cyndi Dale and Richard Wehrman, "Introduction," *The Subtle Body: An Encyclopedia of Your Energetic Anatomy* (Boulder, CO: Sounds True, 2009), xxi.

34. Richard Gerber, *Vibrational Medicine: The #1 Handbook of Subtle-energy Therapies*, 3rd ed. (Rochester, VT: Bear, 2001), 52.

35. Ibid., 68.

36. Ibid., 121.

37. "Psychoenergetics—William Tiller Ph.D." *YouTube*, www.liloumace.com, 15 Oct. 2012, Web, 31 May 2014.

38. Cyndi Dale, *The Subtle Body: An Encyclopedia of Your Energetic Anatomy* (Boulder, CO: Sounds True, 2009), 13.

39. Ibid., 401.

40. Ibid., 402.

41. Cam Dawson, "Dawson Program Principles," *Vibrational Kinesiology*, Web, 9 Sept. 2014, <http://vibrationalkinesiology.com>.

42. Cameron Dawson, *Secrets of Health Revealed: A Synopsis of the Electro-physical Features of the Human Boy and Their Relationship to Human Health*, Dawson Program (2004), 21.

43. Ibid., 18.

44. Ibid., 14.

45. Ibid., 12.

46. Ibid., 13.

Bibliography

"About Chronic Disease." *National Health Council.* 29 July
2014. Web. 17 Nov. 2014.

Alexander, Eben. *Proof of Heaven: A Neurosurgeon's Journey
into the Afterlife.* Sydney: Pam Macmillan Australia,
2012.

"An Agricultural Testament—Albert Howard—ToC."
*Journey to Forever: Hong Kong to Cape Town Overland—An
Adventure in Environment and Development, Join Us on the
Internet, All Welcome, Participation, Online Education, School
Projects, Free of Charge.* Web. 23 Aug. 2011. <http://
journeytoforever.org/farm_library/howardAT/
ATtoc.html>.

Backster, Cleve. *Primary Perception: Biocommunication with
Plants, Living Foods and Human Cells.* Anza, CA: White
Rose Millennium, 2003.

Balfour, Lady Eve. *The Living Soil.* Soil Association,
2006: 46.

"BBC—KS3 Bitesize Science—Magnets and Electric
Current: Revision, Page 3." *BBC—Homepage.*

British Broadcasting Corporation. Web. 20 June 2013. <http://www.bbc.co.uk/bitesize/ks3/science/energy_electricity_forces/magnets_electric_effects/revision/3/>.

Berger, S. L., T. Kouzarides, R. Shiekhattar, and A. Shilatifard. "An Operational Definition of Epigenetics." *Genes Development*: 781–83.

"Blue Light Has a Dark Side." *Harvard Health Publications*. Harvard Medical School, 1 May 2012. Web. 16 Jan. 2015.

Brunetti, Jerry. "Pasture Diversity the Spice of Life for Livestock Health." *Australian Farm Journal* 2010: 25–35.

Childre, Doc Lew, and Mike Atkinson. *Science of the Heart: Exploring the Role of the Heart*. Boulder Creek, CA: HeartMath Research Center, Institute of HeartMath, 2001.

Chopra, Deepak. "Healing." I Can Do It Conference. Hay House Australia. Melbourne Convention Centre, Melbourne. 6 Aug. 2011. Keynote Speech.

Clynes, Dr Manfred. "About Sentic Cycles." Sentic Cycles. Web. 25 Feb. 2015. <http://senticcycles.org>.

Clynes, Dr Manfred. "On Music and Healing." Sentic Cycles. Web. 25 Feb. 2015. <http://senticcycles.org/home/sentics/articles/somatics.pdf>.

Clynes, Dr Manfred. "Sentics: The Touch of Emotions."
  Sentic Cycles. Web. 25 Feb. 2015. <http://senticcycles.
  org/home/sentics/articles/sentics.pdf>.

Clynes, Dr Manfred. "Sentic Cycles - the Passions at
  Your Fingertips." *Psychology Today* (1972). *Rex Research.*
  Web. 2 Dec. 2014. <http://www.rexresearch.com/
  clynsens/clynes.htm#pt72>.

Cousins, Norman. *Anatomy of an Illness as Perceived by the
  Patient.* New York: WW Norton, 2005.

Dalal, R.C., W.M. Strong, E.J. Weston, and J. Gaffney.
  "Sustaining Multiple Production Systems. Soil
  Fertility Decline and Restoration of Cropping Lands
  in Sub Tropical Queensland." *Tropical Grasslands* 25
  (1991): 173–80.

Dale, Cyndi. *The Subtle Body: An Encyclopedia of Your Energetic
  Anatomy.* Boulder, CO: Sounds True, 2009.

Davies, C. Glyn. "Design and Justification Statement,
  No 23 Royal Crescent, Bath." *Bath and North
  East Somerset Council.* 14 June 2012. Web. 8 Jan.
  2015. <http://www.bathnes.gov.uk/WAM/doc/
  BackGround Papers-590820.pdf?extension=.
  pdf&id=590820&location=VOLUME2&
  contentType=application/
  pdf&pageCount=1&appid=1001>.

Dawson, Cam. "Dawson Program Principles." *Vibrational Kinesiology.* Web. 9 Sept. 2014. <http://vibrationalkinesiology.com>.

Dawson, Cameron. *Secrets of Health Revealed: A Synopsis of the Electro-physical Features of the Human Boy and Their Relationship to Human Health.* Dawson Program, 2004.

"Descartes, René: Overview [Internet Encyclopedia of Philosophy]." *Internet Encyclopedia of Philosophy.* Web. 19 Mar. 2013. <http://www.iep.utm.edu/descarte/>.

Diamond, John. *Your Body Doesn't Lie: How to Increase Your Life Energy through Behavioral Kinesiology.* New York: Warner, 1980.

Diamond, John. *Life Energy.* New York: Dodd, Mead, 1985.

"Electromagnetic Spectrum Diagram." *MY NASA DATA.* National Aeronautics and Space Administration. Web. 2 Dec. 2014. <http://mynasadata.larc.nasa.gov/science-processes/electromagnetic-diagram/>.

Elert, Glenn. "Frequency Range of Dog Hearing." *Hypertextbook.com.* Web. 20 Feb. 2012. <http://hypertextbook.com/facts/2003/TimCondon.shtml>.

Emoto, Masaru. *The Hidden Messages in Water.* New York, NY: Atria, 2005.

Fallon, Sally. "Francis M. Pottenger, MD." *Weston A Price.* 1 Jan. 2000. Web. 2 Dec. 2014. <http://www.westonaprice.org/health-topics/ francis-m-pottenger-md/>.

Fallon, Sally, and Mary G. Enig. *Nourishing Traditions: The Cookbook That Challenges Politically Correct Nutrition and the Diet Dictocrats.* Rev. 2nd ed. Washington, DC: NewTrends Pub., 2001.

"Fertilizer Consumption and Grain Production for the World, 1950–2013." *Earth Policy Institute.* Earth Policy Institute, 8 Jan. 2014. Web. 6 Jan. 2015. <http://www. earth-policy.org/data_center/C24>.

Food, Inc. Alliance Vivafilm, 2008. DVD.

Gerber, Richard. *Vibrational Medicine: The #1 Handbook of Subtle-energy Therapies.* 3rd ed. Rochester, VT: Bear, 2001.

"Golden Ratio." *Math Is Fun—Maths Resources.* Web. 16 July 2013. <http://www.mathsisfun.com/numbers/ golden-ratio.html>.

Gray, Richard. "Phobias May Be Memories Passed down in Genes from Ancestors." *The Sydney Morning Herald.* 3 Dec. 2013. Web. 13 Dec. 2013. <http://www.smh. com.au/lifestyle/life/phobias-may-be-memories- passed-down-in-genes-from-ancestors-20131202- 2ymh5.html>.

"Holism And Evolution." *Internet Archive: Digital Library of Free Books, Movies, Music; Wayback Machine.* Web. 30 Aug. 2011. <http://www.archive.org/stream/holismandevoluti032439mbp#page/n9/mode/2up>.

Howard, Sir Albert. "Introduction." *An Agricultural Testament.* London: Oxford UP, 1943.

Jones, Dr. Christine. "Soil carbon sequestration—the science on farm". RCS International Conference. Royal on the Park, Brisbane, Australia. 20 July 2010. Keynote Speech.

Jones, Dr Christine. "The Magic of Carbon." ExecutiveLink and GrowthLink Forums. Resource Consulting Services. Shearwater Resort, Caloundra, Queensland, Australia. 9 Mar. 2011. Keynote Speech.

Keats, Brian, and Stefan Mager. *Biodynamic Growing: Healthcare for Earth and Humanity.* 2nd Extended ed. Mullumbimby, N.S.W.: Aracariaguides, 2009.

Larsen, Janet. "Grain Harvest." *Eco-Economy Indicators - Grain Harvest | EPI.* Earth Policy Institute, 17 Jan. 2013. Web. 2 Dec. 2014. <http://www.earth-policy.org/indicators/C54>.

"Life Archives - Phi 1.618: The Golden Number." *Phi 1618 The Golden Number.* 1 Jan. 2012. Web. 21 Jan. 2015. <http://www.goldennumber.net/category/life/>.

Lipton, Bruce. *The Biology of Belief.* 12th ed. New York: Hay House, 2010.

McCance, Robert Alexander, and Elsie May Widdowson. *McCance and Widdowson's: The Composition of Foods: Sixth Summary Edition.* 06, 6th Summary ed. Cambridge: Royal Society of Chemistry, 2002.

MacManaway, Dr Patrick. "Quantum Leap Workshop Level 1." RCS Quantum Leap Workshop Series. Resource Consulting Services. Rydges International Resort, Yeppoon, Queensland, Australia. 24 Nov. 2010. Class Lecture.

MacManaway, Dr Patrick. "Quantum Leap Workshop Level 2." RCS Quantum Leap Workshop Series. Resource Consulting Services. Bardon Conference Centre, Brisbane, Queensland, Australia. 11 Mar. 2012. Lecture.

MacManaway, Dr Patrick. "What are subtle energies and how do they work?" RCS International Conference. Resource Consulting Services. Royal on the Park, Brisbane, Australia. 21 July 2010. Lecture.

McCraty, Rollin, Mike Atkinson, and Dana Tomasino. "Molulation of DNA Conformation by Heart Focused Intelligence." *Institute of Heart Math.* Web. 17 July 2013. <www.heartmath.org/templates/ihm/downloads/pdf/research/publications/modulation-of-dna.pdf>.

McCraty, Rolin, Mike Atkinson, Dana Tomasino, and Raymond Bradley. *The Coherent Heart*. Boulder: Institute of Heart Math, 2006.

Mager, Stefan. *Permaculture Guide*. Mullumbimby, N.S.W.: Aracariaguides.

Michael Atkin. ABC television, Brisbane, Australia. 11 Dec. 2012. Web. Transcript.

Moeller, Rachael. "Study Suggests Common Knee Surgery's Effect Is Purely Placebo." *Scientific American Global RSS*. 12 July 2002. Web. 5 Sept. 2014. <http://www.scientificamerican.com/article/study-suggests-common-kne/>.

"Mohamed Hijri: A Simple Solution to the Coming Phosphorus Crisis." *TED: Ideas worth Spreading*. Web. 21 Nov. 2013. <http://www.ted.com/talks/mohamed_hijri_a_simple_solution_to_the_coming_phosphorus_crisis.html>.

Montgomery, Paul. "Rene Dubos, Scientist and Writer, Dead." *New York Times* 21 Feb. 1982. *NYTimes.com*. Web. 9 Jan. 2014. <http://www.nytimes.com/1982/02/21/obituaries/rene-dubos-scientist-and-writer-dead.html>.

Murray, Robert K. "Carbohydrates of Physiological Significance." *Harper's Biochemistry*. 24th ed. Stamford, Ct.: Appleton & Lange, 1996. Print.

"National Chronic Diseases Strategy." Australian Government Department of Health and Ageing, 1 Jan. 2006. Web. 10 Oct. 2014.

"Natural Intelligence and the Heart with Joseph Chilton Pearce." Interview.

Nugent, Dr. Steve. *The Missing Nutrients.* Second ed. Scottsdale, Texas: Alethia Corporation, 2006.

Pert, Candace B. *Molecules of Emotion: Why You Feel the Way You Feel.* New York, NY: Scribner, 1997.

Pollan, Michael. *The Omnivore's Dilemma: The Search for a Perfect Meal in a Fast-food World.* London: Bloomsbury, 2007.

"Population Estimates | Ecology Global Network." *Ecology Global Network.* Ecology Global Network, 21 Sept. 2011. Web. 6 Jan. 2015. <http://www.ecology. com/population-estimates-year-2050/>.

Pottenger, Francis. *Pottenger's Cats: A Study in Nutrition.* Second ed. Lemon Grove, California: Price-Pottenger Nutrition Foundation Incorporated, 1995.

Principles of Healthy Diets. Washington DC: Weston A Price Foundation, 2010.

"Psychoenergetics—William Tiller Ph.D." *YouTube.* Www. liloumace.com, 15 Oct. 2012. Web. 31 May 2014. <https://www.youtube.com/watch?v=pI7jO1JuF-c>.

Rollins, Dr John. "Gyconutrients: The Most Controversial Discovery in Modern Health Care." *The Atlanta Voice* 1 Mar. 2010.

Savory, Allan. "How to green the world's deserts and reverse climate change." TED Talks. TED, Long Beach, California. 1 Feb. 2013. Lecture.

"Sherry Strong—The Consumption Concept—Nature's Guide to a Healthy Relationship with Food." *Nutri-Tech Solutions.* Web. 24 Aug. 2011. <http://www.ntshealth.com.au/wellness/video/sherry-strong-the-consumption-concept.html>.

Smith, Timothy K. "Manfred Clynes Sees A Pattern in Love—He's Got the Printouts." *Home.* Web. 16 July 2013. <http://www.microsoundmusic.com/page21.html?bpid=8881>.

Smuts, Jan Christiaan. *Holism and Evolution.* Repr. ed. Westport, Conn.: Greenwood, 1973.

Solar Revolution. Perf. Dieter Broers, Richard Sheldrake. Screen Addiction, 2012. DVD.

Story of the Price-Pottenger Nutrition Foundation. Morley Video Productions, 2007. Film.

Teverberg, Gail. "A Worrying Look At World Energy Consumption Since 1820 | Business Insider Australia." *Business Insider Australia | Business News, Trends and Insights.* 15 Mar. 2012. Web. 12 June 2013.

<http://au.businessinsider.com/a-worrying-look-at-world-energy-consumption-since-1820-2012-3>.

"The Electromagnetic Spectrum—Index Page." *The Electromagnetic Spectrum—Index Page*. NASA. Web. 4 Oct. 2014. <http://science.hq.nasa.gov/kids/imagers/ems/>.

The Language of the Divine Matrix. Distributed by Source Books, Inc., 2007. Film.

"The Parthenon and Phi, the Golden Ratio." Phi 1618 The Golden Number. 20 Jan. 2013. Web. 7 Jan. 2015. <http://www.goldennumber.net/parthenon-phi-golden-ratio/>.

"The Price-Pottenger Story." *YouTube*. YouTube, 3 July 2007. Web. 5 Feb. 2014. <http://www.youtube.com/watch?v=XPCOGSnjP5w>.

"The Science of Peace—The Documentary." *The Science of Peace*. Web. 20 June 2013. <http://www.scienceofpeace.com/document.html>.

Thomas, David. "A Study on the Mineral Depletion of Foods Available to Us as a Nation over the Period 1940 to 1991." *Mineral Resources International (UK) Ltd*. 1 Jan. 2000. Web. 24 Nov. 2014. <http://www.mineralresourcesint.co.uk/pdf/mineral_deplet.pdf>.

Tompkins, Peter, and Christopher Bird. *The Secret Life of Plants*. [1st ed. New York: Harper & Row, 1973.

Tortora, Gerard J., and Bryan Derrickson. "The Special Senses." *Principles of Anatomy and Physiology.* 13th ed. New York: Wiley, 2012. 642.

Trappe, J. "A.B. Frank and Mycorrhizae: The Challenge to Evolutionary and ecologic theory. [Mycorrhiza. 2005] - PubMed Result." *National Center for Biotechnology Information.* Web. 10 July 2011. <http://www.ncbi.nlm. nih.gov/pubmed/15503185>.

Yang, Yang. "Trends in US Adult Chronic Disease Mortality, 1960-1999:Age, Period and Cohort Variations." *US National Library of Medicine National Institute of Health.* 1 May 2008. Web. 17 Nov. 2014. <http://www.ncbi.nlm.nih.gov/p   mycorrhizal mycorrhizal/articles/PMC2831365/>.